REASON AND
MORALS

REASON AND MORALS

BY

JOHN WILSON

CAMBRIDGE

AT THE UNIVERSITY PRESS

1961

PUBLISHED BY
THE SYNDICS OF THE CAMBRIDGE UNIVERSITY PRESS

Bentley House, 200 Euston Road, London, N.W. 1
American Branch: 32 East 57th Street, New York 22, N.Y.
West African Office: P.O. Box 33, Ibadan, Nigeria

©

CAMBRIDGE UNIVERSITY PRESS

1961

Printed in Great Britain at the University Press, Cambridge
(Brooke Crutchley, University Printer)

CONTENTS

PREFACE

THIS book was written against the rather hectic background that surrounds every housemaster at a public school: and I am not sure that this has been altogether a disadvantage. There are times when philosophy needs to retire amidst dreaming spires: but there are other times when it needs to learn from roaring boys. For unlike the revolutions in physics and psychology of this century, the revolution in philosophy has so far failed to make any serious impact outside the universities: and this may be partly because philosophers have not permeated society as scientists and psychologists have done. They have succeeded neither in teaching society the importance of their trade, nor perhaps in learning from society those things that would make their trade more important still. Indeed it sounds naïve even to claim that philosophy is as directly and immediately important to the lives of communities and individuals as science and psychology are. Yet I sincerely believe that it is, and also that some modern philosophers have been too hesitant in saying why and how it is. Hence this book.

ACKNOWLEDGEMENTS

I should like to thank all those who have helped me with advice and criticism: in particular Professor R. B. Braithwaite, Dr F. J. Shirley, Mr J. G. King, Mr and Mrs C. H. Rieu, and, above all, my wife.

J. B. W.

CHAPTER I

THE VALUE OF MORAL PHILOSOPHY

I. WHAT MORAL PHILOSOPHERS DO

THE positivist movement in philosophy has now had over thirty years in which to develop, expand, and recapitulate. Philosophers who have been influenced by this movement are now not only regarded as intellectually and socially respectable, at least in academic and highbrow circles, but may even be said to exercise a dominant influence in many parts of the world. In England and Scandinavia this influence amounts to a virtual monopoly. In the U.S.A. and the British Commonwealth it is immensely strong, though not without competitors. Yet moral philosophers of this persuasion must be aware that a large proportion of their reading public finds their work disappointing and unsatisfying; and it is remarkable, to say the least, that in an age of easy communication it should not carry more weight and be more fully understood in such countries as France and Germany. It is natural, for anyone who (like myself) is sufficiently sympathetic with this kind of philosophy to desire its expansion rather than its extinction, to ask why this should be so.

Yet the answer is not easy; and because it is not easy, we may feel tempted to follow those thinkers who dismiss it as sterile and unfruitful, as 'just playing around with words', or even as a sort of giant academic hoax.[1] Wholesale dismissal of any school of philosophy, however, is so

---

[1] E.g. Ernest Gellner in *Words and Things* (Gollancz, 1959).

I

plainly unjustifiable that we should be wiser to persist with the question. Again, we may feel simply that these philosophers are bad at publicity, so to speak: that they have been incompetent at making their points clear to the general public. But when we consider how limpidly comprehensible are the writings of Professor Ayer, for instance, when compared with almost any contemporary German or French metaphysician, it is plain that this answer will not do either. Modern moral philosophers do not disappoint their general public by being so obviously wrong-headed and absurd that they can be dismissed wholesale, nor by being so incomprehensible that the reader gives up in despair. They disappoint in a much more emotional way: as a parent can disappoint a child, not as a crossword puzzle can disappoint someone who does not understand the clues. The public feels let down: it is almost as if the philosophers had not kept some kind of tacit and long-standing promise. But in what particular way does the public feel disappointed, and whose fault is it? What is it that they expect, and do they have a right to expect it from philosophers? We can only answer such questions by a more detailed investigation.

Nearly all of these philosophers would agree in rejecting the traditional view of moral philosophy, in so far as it entails the belief that the philosopher should tell people, by direct injunction or advice, what moral principles they should adopt or what type of life they ought to choose. The philosopher may investigate, but should not advertise, conclusions such as 'The contemplative life is the best', 'Act only from a sense of duty', 'Always bring about the greatest happiness of the greatest number', and so on. As Nowell-Smith says of 'questions in the form "What shall I do?"', no general answer can be given to this type

2

of question.[1] The philosopher, then, refuses to legislate for men in general. Nor, *a fortiori*, does he consider himself entitled to legislate for any particular man or group of men. For what a man or a group of men ought to do at any particular moment depends at least in part on a great variety of factual or empirical considerations concerning which the philosopher cannot be expected to have any expert knowledge. Even if he did have such knowledge, whether relating to the general human condition or to particular cases, he would still not feel qualified to recommend in his capacity as philosopher. For there are no logical or epistemological reasons why any set of empirical facts should compel anyone to adopt any particular principle or to make any particular moral judgement.

Before the end of the last century it was believed by most people, including professional philosophers, that the job of the moral philosopher was primarily to make moral recommendations with a view to action: to influence men to live differently. This belief has had a long and virtually uninterrupted history, and has been held even by philosophers who have gone to great pains to clarify and analyse moral language, and to describe the moral concepts and opinions of others. They believed that such clarification and description was a necessary means to the end of moral recommendation. Thus Aristotle devotes a great deal of

[1] See P. H. Nowell-Smith's *Ethics* (Pelican edition, 1954), perhaps the best work written from the modern standpoint, which contains numerous indications of this point of view. He writes (pp. 319–20): 'The most a moral philosopher can do is to paint a picture of various types of life in the manner of Plato and ask which type of life you really want to lead. But this is a dangerous task to undertake....In cases which are difficult to decide it is vain to try to answer...without a knowledge both of psychology and of the individual case.' And later: 'The questions "What shall I do?" and "What moral principles should I adopt?" must be answered by each man for himself.'

1-2

space to what would now be called the analysis of ethical terms, or 'logical geography', and a great deal to the description of current views on moral problems; but he firmly maintains that the object of ethics is to produce a change in human action. This view is shared by philosophers as widely differing as Plato and Bentham, Epicurus and Kant, St Thomas Aquinas and John Stuart Mill; and it is implied, where it is not openly stated, by the work of almost every ethical philosopher who has ever written.

More recently, however, this view has been denied: though for the most part less explicitly denied than it had previously been explicitly stated. Modern philosophers do not think that the philosopher is entitled to make moral recommendations in his professional capacity. He is not more likely to be right than anyone else: the extent of his ability to solve moral problems correctly is not to be measured by his merits as a philosopher. This movement has from its inception tended to place very much more stress on logic, epistemology and the philosophy of science than upon ethics. However the movement may have influenced contemporary thought in other ways, this emphasis of interest still pertains today. It is only recently that the positivist attempts to remove metaphysics and ethics from the philosophical arena altogether have been seen to be misjudged; there is still a general unwillingness to admit the work of the ethical philosopher even within its proper limits.

But if the philosopher is neither particularly wise in the ways of the world nor an expert on matters of empirical fact—if he is neither sage nor scientist—how is his work to be described? Philosophers themselves are accustomed to speak of philosophical statements as being 'second-order' statements. Thus, an actual moral judgement or moral principle is made in a 'first-order' statement: that which is written about this judgement or principle, or the statement which expresses it, is written in 'second-order' statements. The metaphor has also been used of a two-storey building, in which ordinary people carry on their everyday business and conversation on the ground floor, while philosophers observe this business and conversation from a bird's-eye view on the first floor.

These descriptions certainly give us a fair approximation of the philosopher's position *vis-à-vis* the rest of the world: a position which, we may observe, if it is not precisely as god-like as that of the philosopher-sage who is now out of fashion, is almost equally remote. But it is only an approximation; for there are many different kinds of second-order statement: many different ways in which those on the first floor may comment upon the activities of those at ground level. If a man on the ground floor says, for example, 'All men are born equal' we can imagine various replies by another ground-floor occupant: 'You're quite right: down with Apartheid!', 'None of that radical nonsense!', 'Certainly not, everyone's different', and so on. But we may equally imagine different second-order comments: by a historian, 'In the past this egalitarian view has been the expression of a protest against tyranny, the historical consequences of which in North America have been. . .'; by a psychologist, 'The demand for equality with other individuals arises chiefly in extropunitives, whose unrationalised aggressive tendencies (probably due to lack of security in infancy) have. . .'; or by a philosopher, 'Although this statement may look like an indicative statement of empirical fact, it is more likely to be a statement of attitude or a concealed value-judgement: for if we try to verify...'. What is common to the second-order comments seems to be that the speakers do not agree or disagree with the original statement, but approach it from the point of view of their particular expertise: historical, psychological, or philosophical.

The nature of second-order philosophical activity, as opposed to other forms of second-order activity, is often described as 'linguistic': but it would be more accurate to say that it is concerned primarily with questions of meaning and verification, or more generally with questions of logic and epistemology. And here we may observe that philosophers do not (or need not) entirely fail to live up to the traditional view of the philosopher as the Guide to Truth. It is beliefs and statements that are true, and not things: and for a statement to be true, we must first be clear about what it means and how to verify it. It is in this sense that the philosopher is interested chiefly in logic and epistemology: the satisfaction of the second condition of truth—whether or not there is actually good evidence for the statement—he leaves to other people.

A very important part of the philosopher's work consists in commenting not so much upon the statements made on the ground floor, but upon the statements of his fellow-workers on the first floor. Returning to our examples of first-floor comments above, we can imagine the philosopher saying to the historian: 'What exactly do you mean by "tyranny" in this context?', or to the psychologist: 'How do you verify whether a man is an "extropunitive", and what empirical evidence have you for putting this down to infantile insecurity?' It seems, indeed, as if our metaphor of a two-storey building is too simple, and that the philosopher speaks from a higher level than anyone else, in a way which can only be commented upon by another philosopher working on the same level. It is true that if a philosopher can patronise a historian by writing a philosophy of history, the historian can retort by writing a history of philosophy; and of course there is no doubt that the writings of philosophers, at least in the past, form as good subject-matter for psychological analysis as anything else. But the philosopher still seems to occupy a particularly god-like position. His logical comments upon young sciences such as psychology may be considered valuable; but one doubts whether any useful purpose would be achieved by psychological analysis of, for example, Ayer's *Language, Truth and Logic*, or Strawson's *Introduction to Logical Theory*.

Speaking still within our vague and approximate description of philosophical activity, we may say that the philosopher's business is to make second-order statements whenever these help to clarify first-order knowledge. When first-order knowledge is progressing satisfactorily, the philosopher retires. In the past, for instance, philosophy included what we should now call science; but as soon as the methodology of science becomes established, the philosopher loses some of his importance. The methodology is today firmly established; and the philosopher is now interested chiefly in those difficulties of meaning and verification which arise whenever the boundaries of science extend and the meaning of scientific statements becomes questionable in consequence. Thus, the philosopher is interested in the concepts of 'unconscious desire' and of 'thinking machines', because it is not altogether clear what logical role is played by these concepts in scientific theory.

Now this looks as if the philosopher's activity might be very useful. We have, perhaps, a picture of the philosopher

7

as a kind of logical fairy godmother, who steps in and solves the problems of meaning and verification whenever these impede the progress of first-order knowledge, or a universal aunt who rears the growing sciences in their infancy, and sends them down the royal road of logic with her blessing. The ground-floor workers come to the philosopher and say: 'We are very sorry, but we do not know what we are talking about. Can you tell us, please, so that we can get on with the job?'; and the philosopher benignly answers: 'Yes, you mean so-and-so, and the sort of evidence you want for your statements is such-and-such; now I shall go upstairs for a rest, and watch your future progress with interest.' But in point of historical fact this does not seem to happen. What seems to happen is that the philosopher arrives on the scene several centuries too late, and explains the advance of knowledge *post eventum*. He approaches the scientist and says: 'Do you know why your studies have prospered so well? It is because you have decided to accept the observations of sense-experience as your method of verification; and on this basis you have built up a fine, sophisticated and useful corpus of knowledge.' The scientist, who is a busy man, replies: 'Well, thank you, that is very nice to know: now if you will excuse me I must make some more of the observations you have mentioned.' The philosopher seems to be not so much a universal aunt as a sort of universal tidier-up. He can only tell us why we know something when we already know it. And according to this second picture we might well say of philosophy, as Socrates says of Polemarchus' idea of justice in Plato's *Republic*, that it is 'not really worth taking seriously'.

These are more like caricatures than pictures, of course; but we should still prefer to believe that the first was more lifelike than the second. To put this point in another way: philosophers sometimes talk about 'philosophical doubt' and the way in which they endeavour to resolve it, contrasting it with ordinary doubt in much the same way as second-order problems are contrasted with first-order. The former is that state of mind under whose influence philosophers sometimes say 'This seems queer' or 'There is something (logically) odd about this which I do not understand'. They grope around the logical and linguistic landscape until the doubt evanesces. The latter is the kind of doubt we might feel about the question: 'Is there animal life on Venus?' This kind of doubt seems more real and profitable than the former; it disappears only when we have collected enough empirical evidence to settle it one way or the other. In other words, when ordinary doubt has been resolved, knowledge is advanced; but when the philosophers' doubt has been resolved, how are we better off than we were before? We could think that philosophical doubt acts as an important obstacle to the advance of knowledge, in that until it has been resolved we do not know what empirical questions to ask or how to answer them; that philosophical doubt prevents us from having the ordinary doubt which we ought to have. This would correspond with our first and more optimistic picture of philosophy. Or we could think that philosophic doubt is otiose so far as ordinary knowledge is concerned; that the puzzles which baffle the philosopher are of interest to nobody but himself, and may even be largely of his own making. And this forms part of the gloomier picture. Thus, we may agree with Wittgenstein that philosophical problems arise when language is idling and doing no work; but it remains an open question whether this idle machinery impedes the rest of the machine and

9

could itself be used to advantage, or whether it is merely a harmless curiosity.

Philosophers are naturally unwilling to commit themselves on this question, partly at least because second-order workers usually produce better results if they are not continually pestered with demands for a utilitarian justification for their work. To issue an injunction to them such as 'Pursue only those lines of philosophical study which will advance first-order knowledge' is liable to be largely ineffective, because nobody knows which these lines of study are, not even the philosopher. But there is no reason, I think, why philosophers should resign themselves to being regarded by the general public as of no practical value, or why it should not be made clear what kind of services philosophy has rendered in the past and what it may hope to render in the future. A brief investigation will, I believe, make one point clear: that the root of the trouble lies not in what the philosopher does on the first floor, but in his unwillingness or inability to communicate his findings in a way which will be useful to the ground-floor workers.

We may try to classify under different headings a number of activities in moral philosophy, with examples of each, in order that we may see to what extent they can be said to help the man on the ground floor. In doing this we may be open to the charge of making distinctions without differences; and no doubt it is truer to say that there is one homogeneous activity of philosophising than that there is a subject called moral philosophy made up of a known number of parts. But this cannot be helped; and even if our classification acts only as a list of items, certain points may be established.

(1) *Puzzles and paradoxes.* A philosophical puzzle arises

when something has gone wrong with our use of language. Often this seems to present us with a paradox which we cannot resolve, but both halves of which we wish to accept. Here the philosopher resolves the paradox by putting his finger on the spot where the trouble starts. Thus, people are worried by the conjunction of beliefs (*a*) that we have free will, and (*b*) that all our actions have causes, that our behaviour can be predicted by psychologists, that God knows the future, etc. The philosopher can point out that 'cause' does not imply 'compulsion', that neither cause, prediction, explanation nor anything in the same logical group is in conflict with personal freedom or self-determination, and that therefore this worry is unnecessary.

(2) *Explanation of moral discourse.* By this I refer to the sort of *post eventum* explanation already noticed in reference to the philosophy of science, which makes clear the logical geography lying behind our moral thinking. For instance, most people can distinguish between a virtue and a talent, or between a vice and a misfortune. But most people cannot state the criteria for the distinction accurately. They know, in any particular case, what counts as a moral issue and what does not; but they may need the philosopher's help in giving an answer to the general question 'What makes an issue a moral issue?' Again, most people consider motives in a moral light as well as actions. The philosopher may be able to explain why they do this; and this explanation may help them to pass judgement on difficult cases, such as that of the Inquisitor who commits the most wicked deeds of cruelty from the highest motives. (The philosopher might say, for instance, that our reason for valuing a man with good motives is simply that he is more likely than another to do good actions in the future, even if he has not acted well on one particular occasion:

thus providing us with criteria for assessing the value of motives as against action.)

(3) *Critique of past philosophers*. Without necessarily recommending or condemning the first-order moralising of philosophers in the past, the modern moral philosopher can (and does) spend a great deal of time in examining and elucidating it. This he may do partly from a historical point of view (and here he is writing a history of moral concepts), partly by simple exposition, and partly by submitting the philosopher concerned to a modern interrogation by logical and linguistic methods. As a result of the interrogation many valid and important points of logic and language may emerge, made either by the philosopher himself (perhaps obscurely) or by his critic in the course of criticism.

I do not think that these three types of activity provide us with the optimistic picture of moral philosophy that we hope for. To most people, the puzzles of philosophy have no more intrinsic importance than a chess problem or a crossword puzzle; and similarly, while it may be interesting to know that the distinction between (for instance) vice and misfortune is such-and-such, it seems quite sufficient to be able to distinguish them. Any anxiety generated by these issues is a purely intellectual anxiety, which intellectuals share only with neurotics; a neurotic might be seriously worried by determinism, or by the fact that his actions were predictable, but the sane man knows he is free. Again, the elucidation of the moral precepts of past philosophers seems to have point only if their modern critics are prepared to recommend or condemn them: and this is precisely what they are not willing to do. For the rest, it is merely another logical game for intellectuals with time to waste.

The Value of Moral Philosophy

The logical elucidation coming from these three activities, however, does have considerable value in borderline cases. Nine times out of ten, we know how to distinguish a vice from a misfortune; but the tenth time, when we do not know, our only hope lies in discovering and applying the criteria consciously. A case in point is our worry over the treatment of certain criminals: are certain crimes to be treated as misfortunes, like kleptomania, or as vices, like dishonesty? Again, we may normally find no logical difficulties (though we may often wish to know more facts) about passing moral judgement on a man whose motives and actions are of a certain kind; but occasionally (as with the Inquisitor) we experience logical uncertainty. In cases of this type logical elucidation, whether resulting from a consideration of puzzles and paradoxes, of everyday moral discourse, or of past philosophers, is plainly of value.

But such cases are not very frequent; and if the philosopher limited himself to them, his defence would remain weak. It is true that many of the serious issues currently discussed—capital punishment, artificial insemination, euthanasia, birth control and so on—involve relations between morality, religion, psychology, the criminal law, and other departments of theory and practice; and it is also true that a clarification of the logic of such relations would be of great value. But the use of philosophy seems confined, in practice at least, to those occasions alone when our customary behaviour and customary use of concepts appear to let us down: in other words, to the borderline or awkward cases mentioned above. It is as if philosophers concurred in the general view that there is, by and large, nothing very much wrong with our conceptual tools: that they only occasionally need expert adjustment. We do not seem to get any *lead* from the philosophers, any radical revision produced on their own initiative and not by the pressure of topicality. They are like doctors who cure or palliate our symptoms, but never diagnose a deep-seated disease or suggest a complete physical check-up and overhaul.

Another way of putting this charge would be to say that none of the three sorts of activity mentioned above goes very far towards *changing* our moral judgements, even though they may confirm us in making some of them. Yet the wide divergences on matters of morality and value suggest that some change is required somewhere. The lack of progress towards a reasoned unanimity in moral matters is extremely distressing. The moralising of past philosophers seems to have had no effect, which is hardly surprising in view of the fact that their recommendations differed so widely; but now that moral philosophers have cast off moralising, we may feel entitled to expect from them some kind of rational methodology, so that we may do our own moralising in a reasonable manner. If no such methodology is forthcoming, we should feel that our time was being wasted.

It is possible to give a sort of rough sketch of how the philosopher can satisfy the ordinary man: and this is well worth doing, because phrases like 'second-order recommendations' and 'a new methodology' are unfortunate in that they cut no ice with the ordinary man, and afford a kind of shelter behind which professional philosophers can take refuge from the ordinary man's demands. Somehow modern moral philosophy has become *dry*, and it is essential to bring it back into focus with everyday demands: though, we must hope, without loss of rationality or precision. It is basically as a reaction to this dryness that modern irrationalist philosophies, like existentialism, have arisen and gained popularity. We know that it is always hard for the rational man to gain a hearing: but it ought not to be as hard as philosophers seem to make it.

For the ordinary man the key question is 'How can I tell right from wrong?', or 'How can I tell what I ought to do?' What sort of 'recommendations', then, would help people to answer these questions? Here are some: 'It's just a matter of taste'; 'Ask a psychologist'; 'You needn't bother about justice'; 'Always obey your animal instincts'; 'Forget about morals and concentrate on charity'. Thinkers and religious leaders who were not philosophers in the strict sense, such as Jesus, Bentham, Gandhi, D. H. Lawrence and Freud, managed to change moral thinking by issuing such recommendations. Modern philosophers reject such a method, on the ground that it is biased: why should a philosopher issue imperatives of this sort? What right has he to persuade people into adopting his particular values? But, though such recommendations may be made without the support of reason, *they may also follow as the end product of a piece of philosophical work in the strict sense of 'philosophical'*. I do not mean that any moral proposition can follow logically from a consideration merely of empirical fact or of language: nevertheless, it may follow rationally.

To take a parallel, does the psychoanalyst 'talk you into' changing your values and behaviour? In a sense he does not: that is, he does not persuade, propagandise, or indoctrinate—he does not even exhort. He merely interprets, listens, suggests, and clarifies. But in another sense, of course, he does 'talk you into' changing: that is, he indirectly suggests new categories of thinking. Some ways of thinking come to seem silly (neurotic), and others more important. The philosopher too, as Socrates is supposed once to have suggested, acts as a kind of midwife to thought: by his clarification of concepts some categories of conscious thought appear less useful or less reasonable, and he can suggest new categories to replace them. He may thus achieve the same result as those thinkers and religious leaders quoted above—by reasoning and intellectual clarification, not by playing upon the feelings or emotions. He makes it clear to us what work our concepts—'justice', 'morality', 'freedom' and so on—are actually doing. Often they are not doing the work we think they are: sometimes they are doing no work at all.

It is a pity that psychoanalysis (or any form of depth psychology) does not appear to attract the professional interest of very many philosophers, because the parallel between the two disciplines is really remarkably close. Descriptions by philosophers of 'philosophic doubt'— having a sort of 'mental cramp', being like 'a fly in a bottle' who does not know the way out, not knowing how to set about answering a question—are just like descriptions of neurosis: and it is no accident that both philosophers and psychologists describe their work as 'analysis'.[1] Unfortunately, a good deal of analytic work has to be done on the opinions of past philosophers: which suggests that it is not only, or even chiefly, the conceptual thinking of the ordinary man which is at fault. Indeed, there are plainly metaphysicians whose work looks very like the result of some kind of failure to accept and adjust to reality. We may put them down, if we can temporarily claim the right to this kind of criticism, as intellectuals who have failed to accept the limitations of human

[1] On this subject see John Wisdom's *Philosophy and Psychoanalysis* (Blackwell, 1953).

life: people who want life, and human understanding, to be other (and better) than they can possibly or logically be. They may project their dissatisfaction by irrational belief in a god, angels, ideal forms, and so on: or they may ask questions like 'Are physical objects really there?', 'What's it all for?' or 'Can we ever really know anything?' in a way which suggests that they are psychically involved in these questions, and do not merely regard them as interesting and instructive logical puzzles or paradoxes.

This picture of philosophical problems as the sophisticated man's form of neurosis, and of the modern analytic philosopher as the sophisticated psychiatrist, is illuminating in certain respects, however far it may fall short of a perfect analogy. Quite apart from the fact that it offers a useful description of the actual workings of philosophy, it has two important lessons to teach the moral philosopher. First, he must accept the likelihood that a good deal of our moral thinking is irrational and unhealthy, just as the psychiatrist accepts the fact that most people (not only his patients) fall far short of emotional health. Whole concepts and categories of thought, deeply engrained into our minds and our usage, may be misplaced or mistaken. Secondly, he must nevertheless in some sense do justice even to the grossest aberration, in the same way that the psychiatrist has to take into account every symptom and expression of the patient, simply because they are parts of the patient's personality. In other words, he cannot just write off human concepts, feelings, language or categories of thought: he cannot repress them or abolish them: he has to put them to their proper use. Conceptual ill-health, like emotional maladjustment, consists in the misuse, or misplacement, or misunderstanding of concepts and feelings. They must be put into proportion, saved from neurotic conflict with each other, reshaped and dovetailed.

Thus, for a philosopher to use the ordinary man's feelings and language as a norm is in one way correct, and in another mistaken. It is correct to use them as a norm, in the sense that he must not seek simply to override or destroy them (as a misguided psychologist or doctor might seek to solve the sexual problems of a patient by castrating him); he must seek to satisfy the patient. But ordinary feelings and language are not normative in another sense, simply because (*a*) they may be the product of neurosis, and (*b*) even if healthy, they may be being used in the wrong context. Hence the philosopher must be extremely sympathetic in seeking to understand what lies behind them, so that he can see what job they ought to be doing: but quite uncompromising in pointing out where they are being abused, and in showing the irrationalities to which such abuses lead.

2. DOUBTS AND POSSIBILITIES

We have voiced a complaint about the dryness of modern moral philosophy: as if the people had asked for bread, and been given a stone. Of course this may not be the philosopher's fault: the people may have expected manna from Heaven, and the philosopher is not a miracle-worker. But it is important to realise that this dryness, whether inevitable or not, results from points made by modern moral philosophy itself. It is as if philosophy had somehow *finished* with the business of making recommendations of a bread-like and not a stone-like kind: as if it had somehow grown out of bakery and turned to quarrying. To go back to making recommendations, it is thought, would be to put the clock back, to degenerate, to act as if we had not gained a vital piece of terrain. We shall be examining this terrain at some length, so as to see exactly what it looks like and how its acquisition changes our viewpoint.

Men ask 'How can I be certain that my morality is right?' or 'Are there any really good reasons for believing that such-and-such is right?' One way of starting off is to say that this is a demand for a methodology of ethics, and particularly for criteria of ethical certainty. It is not simply a demand to make everyone hold the same moral views, and derive them from the same criteria. If it were simply this, then philosophers might reasonably suggest either that all men should be made to hold the same moral views by a process of indoctrination or psychological manipulation, or that all moral problems should be settled by throwing dice or tossing a coin. Both these suggestions, if adopted, would result in unanimity about morals, and the worry caused by moral disagreement would disappear: but in fact both would be indignantly rejected, or regarded as merely flippant. What is being demanded, then, is some sort of rational and acceptable criteria for moral certainty which will lead to unanimity, but without which unanimity is considered undesirable: certainty, not merely in the sense of feeling certain about moral judgements, but in the sense which entails being *justified* in having that feeling. Again, we can see that if this were not so, the appeal would be made to indoctrinators or educationalists, and not to philosophers. For the philosopher's business includes giving the logical criteria for certainty, but does not include indoctrination.

It is easy to see why the demand has been thought philosophically illegitimate. Words and phrases like 'certainty', 'knowledge', 'justified in thinking that', 'having good reasons for believing that' and so forth are nearly always used in respect of established criteria and methods of verification, and their meaning is nearly always fixed in reference to them. For the vast majority of meaningful propositions, propositions which we know to be true, or about which we are certain, there are agreed and established criteria of truth. Thus, if I say that I am certain that the sun will rise tomorrow, I would justify my being certain by reference to the evidence, criteria or method of verifying the sun's rising tomorrow. Similarly, if I say that I know that an object is pink, I could demonstrate my knowledge by pointing out that I had normal eyesight, that I was looking at it in a good light, that everyone else calls it pink, and that the wavelength of light it gives off, if measured, would be found to correspond with the wavelengths given off by other objects which we call pink. In short, I could demonstrate the truth of my belief by showing that the criteria for pinkness were satisfied. Since everyone accepts these criteria, it follows that the object is pink, and (as a result of my making this claim and of my demonstrating its truth) that I knew it was pink.

If I say 'I am certain that this is a good knife', I mean that I have checked this knife with the agreed criteria for knives being good, that I have done the job thoroughly, and that there is no doubt in my mind that it satisfies these criteria. If I say 'I have good reasons for believing that this is a good knife', I mean that I have checked it with the criteria, done the job fairly thoroughly, and that though some doubt may remain, there is not much doubt that the criteria are satisfied. Going further down the scale of certainty, if I say 'I have reasons for believing that this is a good knife' I probably mean that, though I have not been very thorough, I know that at least some of the most important criteria are satisfied. This analysis is true of moral judgements as well as non-moral ones. If I say 'He is a good man', I may imply criteria which are not universally accepted (as those of knives are): but I imply that they are satisfied nevertheless, and my certainty that the man is good, or my reasons for thinking that he is good, can be analysed in the same way.

This point is not affected by the fact that we often arrange our criteria in a kind of hierarchy. Thus we might approve of a man's resisting the temptation to pick another man's pocket, on the criterion that stealing is bad. But we might defend this criterion in terms of another criterion: we might think stealing bad because it leads to a disordered society. This criterion again, the criterion of whether a society is orderly or disordered, might be defended by a still higher criterion: say, the criterion of whether the members of a society are happy or unhappy. In this case we approve of a man's resisting temptation in a particular instance, because we approve of not stealing: we approve of not stealing because we approve of an orderly society: we approve of an orderly society because we approve of happiness. We have thus a small hierarchy of criteria (or principles, or ends), each of which is justified by the one immediately above it. Whether each criterion is justified is thus a question of fact, to be answered by reference to its immediate superior. Thus we could ask whether respect for private property does, on the whole, lead to an orderly society: or whether an orderly society leads to happiness: and these are factual questions, in the same (logical) way as 'Is this a good knife?' is a factual question, once we know what criterion knives have to satisfy in order to count as good knives.

21

Thus we can verify, by simple and established methods, whether an action or a person or a society lives up to our most immediate criteria for goodness: for instance, whether the action counts as stealing, or the person is dishonest, or the society tyrannical. We could then justify our immediate criteria by higher criteria, and these by still higher criteria. But obviously there is a limit to these justifications. When we come to ultimate criteria, that is, criteria for which we have no higher criteria, we cannot do this. Because for a man to be justifiably certain about anything, or to know anything, there must already be an acceptable method of verification or acceptable criteria for what he is certain about or what he knows. He will use these criteria to prove that he really is certain or really does know, and does not merely believe without reason. On the other hand, where there are no criteria, there can be no certainty and no knowledge. For these words are only comprehensible in reference to established tests, and without the tests it is a basic misunderstanding to ask for certainty or knowledge.

There exists also another argument for the rejection of the demand for certainty in ethics, which it will be well to consider immediately. It is characteristics of words like 'good' and 'ought', whether used in moral contexts or not, that these words are employed to influence choices, to state a preference, to praise and to commend. It has been shown that 'good' retains this element in its meaning irrespective of whether the criteria of goodness are known or not: and it could also be shown that it retains this element whether there actually exist criteria or not. Thus at the end of a moral argument, when two disputants have run out of criteria because they have reached their ultimate criteria, one may say 'I still think your ultimate criteria are not good, and that mine are good'. In such a case, it is plain that the speaker is commending his own criteria, and not commending his disputant's criteria, even though (since the criteria are ultimate) there cannot be higher criteria in terms of which the commendation might be made.

Since this is so, it will always be possible, no matter what the state of ethical knowledge, to say that ultimate criteria are not good: that is, it will always be possible not to commend them and to commend other ultimate criteria. This is true, even if we are in the position of having achieved complete unanimity about morals. Every man in the world might accept the same set of ultimate criteria for his moral judgements, but it would still be logically possible to deny that these criteria were good; for it makes sense to apply the word 'good' simply in order to commend, and without reference to criteria. This is not true in the case of non-moral words like 'pink', because it is not sense to use these words in defiance of, or without reference to, the criteria which form an essential part of their meaning. In other words, the very fact that 'good' can be used simply to commend and that other words cannot, shows that we cannot achieve that certainty in the former case that we can and have achieved in the latter.

This is a point about moral language, or language of value, as opposed to empirical language, or language of description. We can think of analogies. Imagine a green-grocer's shop, in which there are various piles of objects and two sorts of labels stuck on them. One sort says things like 'Apples', 'Cabbages', and so on: the other says '8*d*. a lb.' or '3*s*. each'. Then empirical language is the first sort of label, and evaluative language is the price-tags. The price-tags do not describe or say anything *about* the fruit and vegetables in themselves: they simply price them. Or

23

empirical language is like the features of a roulette board—the individual numbers, the spaces marked 'rouge' and 'noir', and so forth: and evaluative language is like placing a bet on the board—not describing anything, but putting your money on it.

Very well, then: let us not be boring about this: we see the point. So what does the philosopher do about people who ask whether what they think to be right really is right? It is here that we derive the impression that moral philosophy has finished with us. To say 'Yes' or 'No' to a question of this sort, says Professor Ayer, is merely 'to adhere to that particular standpoint'. We cannot justify the standpoint if it is an ultimate standpoint—indeed, surely this is no more than a tautology? 'It is logically absurd to ask a question without knowing how the answers to it are to be judged to be good or bad answers', says Professor Nowell-Smith, driving the point home.[1] All this seems very cosy and watertight.

But, alas! the ineffectiveness of the philosopher to assist in answering questions about ends or ultimate standards can logically be extended to include questions about means or individual cases. Thus, the facts that I approve of the preservation of private property and that this umbrella is Smith's together form a 'good' reason for my not stealing Smith's umbrella. But though it is correct, in point of linguistic usage, to call this a 'good' reason,

[1] Nowell-Smith, *Ethics*, p. 175, where he also writes: '...although we can always question the criteria, there is no practical or logical necessity to do so.' This is precisely what I want to deny. There is a practical necessity, because the vast majority of people demand certainty: they wish to agree, to avoid conflict, to settle arguments. There is a logical necessity, because people actually use, and intend to use (i.e. *mean*), 'good' and other moral words in a way which suggests that there is 'a right answer' which we do not yet know; we call ultimate criteria 'good', but do not know how to judge them good.

it would not be of any use in practice to anybody who was in moral doubt. For moral doubt would necessarily involve questioning the attitude of approval, or questioning its application to this particular case. Any other sort of doubt would be doubt about the empirical facts: and this is not the philosopher's business. It seems, then, that the philosopher's 'good' reasons are only 'good' in cases where the philosopher is not needed.

This looks bad. 'I told you so,' says the suspicious layman, 'you modern philosophers are just sophisticated sceptics. You make out that the whole business of right and wrong is just a matter of taste—just arbitrary: that there is nothing either good or bad, but thinking makes it so.' Certainly the philosopher can try to defend himself against this charge. He can say that morality differs from matters of taste in some way or other—but not in the (to the layman) essential point that there is no way of showing one ultimate morality to be better than another, any more than there is any way of showing dry sherry to be, somehow, better than sweet sherry. He can say that morality is not arbitrary—but only in the sense that we should not be fickle about it, that we should be wise, unprejudiced, open to the facts (but what facts?), and so forth; it remains arbitrary in the all-important sense that it is, ultimately, purely a matter of choice, and there is no way of proving one choice to be better than another. A man may say: 'I have carefully considered all the facts and am quite unprejudiced, and my ultimate standards of morality involve the infliction of pain, death and misery: a world full of sadists and masochists seems to me, after due reflection, wholly admirable: any features of human life which are obviated by such standards appear to me worthless: and I beg of you, please adhere to your particular standpoint and let me adhere to mine.' And the philosopher can do nothing to stop him. This seems queer.

Other doubts also arise. Let us have another look at these 'ultimate criteria'. Suppose *A* holds normal values like happiness, pleasure and sanity, and *B* holds conflicting values (unhappiness, pain, madness), and neither has higher values, then their argument will come to a stop. But does this mean it will have been *settled*? *A* can still sensibly say 'I still think happiness is the right criterion', and *B* can reply 'No, you are wrong, unhappiness is'. And they both put the question 'Is happiness the right criterion or not?', even though (since they had no higher criteria) they would not know how to answer it.[1] What is the philosopher to do with this question? One can think of various possibilities:

(*a*) He can say simply, with Nowell-Smith, that it is 'logically absurd to ask a question without knowing how the answers to it are to be judged good or bad answers'. But somehow this seems unsatisfactory: *A* and *B* could ask 'Is happiness the right criterion or not?'; however 'logically absurd' it may be, it isn't *nonsense* to ask this: and to imply that it is a waste of time to ask it seems rather feeble.

(*b*) He can interpret it as a demand to know which standpoint is held by the person *A* and *B* are addressing— 'Do *you* believe in happiness?' But this won't do: *A* and *B* will say that this isn't what they're asking at all—they're

---

[1] I believe that most people are not content to agree to differ about their ultimate criteria. Though they may admit that they cannot find 'the right answer', they talk and think as if there *was* a right answer. In other words, they do not talk about morals as they talk about 'matters of taste'. On the other hand, it must be admitted that it is logically possible to talk like this, and perhaps some people actually do so consistently. (I have met some who pretend to, but no one who in fact does.)

asking for a justification of the standpoint, not canvassing for another adherent. *A* and *B* are saying '*Ought* one to believe in happiness?' The philosopher can then say, of course, that we don't understand what more could be meant by asking 'Do you think one *ought* to believe...?' than simply 'Do *you* believe...?' But this would be disingenuous: we do understand, even if we do not see how to answer. The philosopher would then have to say, as in (*a*), that it's a waste of time to ask this question since there can be no answer to it: that somehow it must be nonsense: that one ought not to ask it. But this is tyrannical.

(*c*) He can interpret it as a request that some new, potentially higher criterion should be pointed out to *A* and *B*: something which has simply not occurred to them. Thus, to change our example, *A* might believe in not stealing and *B* in grabbing as much money as possible: they might reach an impasse in argument if they were both very naïve, and had always regarded these principles as ultimate. Then, we point out to them that stealing produces social chaos: this might give them a higher criterion than the ones they held at the time, and would perhaps enable them to agree. Here we should simply have put their ultimate criteria down a peg, so to speak, by pointing out to them facts which might carry moral weight: by confronting them with the implications of their criteria. This seems an altogether more profitable proceeding than (*a*) or (*b*): but perhaps it will be said that pointing out facts of this kind is not the philosopher's business, and I do not want to argue the point here.

(*d*) He can interpret it as he might interpret the question 'Is a flying-boat really a boat?', which has this in common with questions about values or moral beliefs, that they are neither of them questions about facts. 'Is a flying-boat a boat or an aeroplane?' seems to call for a *decision* (perhaps in a court of law). So the philosopher could say 'This isn't a question of fact: you must just decide: to ask whether it's *really* a boat is silly, because you have been misled by the grammar of the question into thinking it's a question of fact'. But then that is not very helpful either. *A* and *B* will say 'Yes, we see all that, but we have still got to decide: isn't there anything you can say which may help us?' This seems a reasonable demand: after all, there may be sound and unsound ways of deciding about moral principles, just as there are sound and unsound ways of deciding legal points. So we are forced finally to the last possibility, (*e*).

(*e*) He can interpret the question as a demand to be told the right *ways* to reach moral decisions. He is being asked not as a judge (what decisions are right) but as a teacher of law (what are the criteria for arriving at right decisions). Thus, we might start by saying about the flying-boat 'Well, it depends on what context you take: if you're worried about bomb-dropping, call it an aeroplane: if you're interested in mooring-space, you have to regard it as a boat'. This is some help, at least. The decision gets tied in with human purposes: it gets given *point*. But then it is not really enough: it obviously pays to regard a flying-boat sometimes as a boat and sometimes as an aeroplane, but it looks odd to say that we must sometimes take happiness as a criterion, and sometimes unhappiness. However, *A* and *B* have been given some guidance: they have been told to look at the context and consider human purposes. A lot more work remains to be done: but we have made a start. Interesting and potentially fruitful questions arise, such as 'What sort of contexts do human beings come into?', 'What happens if human purposes conflict?', and 'Can human purposes be misguided?'

We might raise a similar doubt about the way in which some philosophers talk. For instance, what does this talk about 'criteria' add up to? Do people actually use criteria? In the loose sense of 'principles of judgement' no doubt they do: but the whole picture of a neat, snug deductive network of ultimate and subordinate criteria, or ends and means, seems an inappropriate description of how people actually approach moral problems. We might point the contrast by considering a government, or any other authority. A government may fulfil its purposes in two ways which are, in practice, very different. It can adopt a general policy of freedom and tolerance, or it can lay down and establish specific criteria of what actions are to be accounted as tolerable and legitimately free, and what are not. The first method is essentially empiric; if one uses it, one avoids laying down hard and fast rules about what is tolerable and what intolerable, but treats each case on its own merits, as it crops up. The second method is more dogmatic; one lays down rules, and sees that they are obeyed. If a number of hard cases appear, one may come to the decision that one's rules are bad rules, and change them; but this will be a conscious change, and not simply the application of a general policy to cover new cases. In the first instance, we might say that the government had 'principles of judgement', or 'standards', but we would be less likely to say that they had 'criteria', whereas in the second case, 'criteria' is the very word we should want to use.

The description of how most people think about moral issues would be best made in terms of 'policy', 'standards' or 'principles', and not in terms of 'criteria', because their approach to life tends to be empiric. Not many people make a consistent use of anything like a utilitarian calculus. Men often fail to think about why they think things to be good or bad at all; and when they do, they often erect criteria *post eventum*—making the moral judgement first, and erecting the criteria afterwards in accordance with it. Most people, indeed, do not *think* at all in their making of moral judgements: they just make them. Even when they are in doubt, they do not have much use for climbing up and down the ladder of ends and means, or running over the scale of their moral criteria.

It is significant that some moral philosophers misrepresent the way in which ordinary people tackle moral problems, because this *ipso facto* misrepresents the way in which philosophers can be useful to ordinary people. The picture of a network of criteria or ends and means is like an X-ray of an animal, which shows only its general outline. What philosophers have done is to show us the logical skeleton of our moral thinking, demonstrate that there is no question of anybody being logically compelled to have a skeleton of any other shape or material than that which they choose to have, and then leave us to our own devices. But the moral thinking of human beings is more like a very complex and intricate piece of machinery: there are concepts and constellations of concepts, like groups of cog-wheels and levers, and different constellations cope with different problems as they arise in the minds of different people. With *A* a problem may set one particular piece of machinery in operation, with *B* the same problem may give work to quite a different piece.

So the ordinary man might not frame his demand as a demand for certainty about 'ultimate criteria'. He might simply ask for a 'reasonable policy', or 'sensible principles'.

Surely, we might think, some governments, at any rate, have better policies than others: and surely there are ways of verifying this? This demand seems more tolerable, because it is more watered-down. Perhaps, after all, it may be possible to evolve a concept of 'certainty' which does not depend solely upon 'having higher criteria' or 'being verifiable' in the slickly logical way which our previous discussions have suggested to be necessary, but which is yet nothing so irrational as the merely psychological state of 'feeling certain'. Or, we cay say, there might be a way of being 'reasonable' or 'rational' in our moral thinking which entails neither the notion of logical proof, not yet the vague injunctions 'Don't be prejudiced', 'Consider the facts', and so on. It is worth while trying to elucidate this.

Being reasonable consists of (at least) two things, besides being able to argue logically. First, it involves a refusal to be doctrinaire. This refusal implies rather more than an absence of prejudice, more even than a willingness to consider the facts. It suggests a desire to treat each case on its own merits, the ability to learn by experience and to be aware when one lacks appropriate experience, a certain imaginative sympathy or insight into the minds and hearts of other people, and a mental flexibility which enables one to deal with varying problems of varying complexity. I am not suggesting that the philosopher can be of enormous help here, though I do think that good philosophers are not doctrinaire in this sense: for no mind which cuts itself off, either intellectually or emotionally, from other minds can hope to advance very far. Secondly, however, being reasonable consists of having a proper view of human beings and their situation, which can only be enjoyed by somebody who uses efficient conceptual tools. It is not enough merely to be sympathetic: we must also use categories of thought, a language and a methodology which suit reality. It is the philosopher's business to provide us with these tools.

Suppose that a schoolmaster has to deal with a boy who has broken some important rule, and suppose further that the boy is particularly sensitive, so that we agree that punishment would harm him. Then the schoolmaster might do various things:

(*a*) He might refuse to look at the psychological facts about the boy, and punish him in order to satisfy the dictates of retributive justice.

(*b*) He might be willing to look at the facts, but nevertheless give him some punishment—perhaps reluctantly— in the interests of justice.

(*c*) He might *merely* look at the facts, and either punish him in the interests of keeping law and order generally, or not punish him at all.

These various courses are symptomatic of ways in which the schoolmaster might think it right to approach this particular moral problem. How far we think any way 'reasonable' will depend largely on the two components of 'being reasonable' mentioned above. Thus, the refusal to give weight to psychological facts in (*a*) counts against his reasonableness, because this is doctrinaire. In (*b*) he looks at the facts, but the case has engaged a particular part of his moral mechanism—his concept of justice. In (*c*) this concept is not engaged. Which of these approaches we consider more reasonable will depend on whether we think the concept is an efficient tool, or whether we think that it is the right tool to use for this particular piece of work. Here, then, it is of no use to say 'Consider the facts' or 'Be sympathetic': these pieces of advice are neutral as between (*b*) and (*c*). Indeed, if the schoolmaster took course (*a*), he would probably regard the advice as irrelevant in this case also: for in (*a*) the *only* part of the mechanism that is engaged is the concept of justice. This, he thinks, is a job which this concept can do by itself: and the fact that the boy is sensitive may seem to him as irrelevant to the problem as the fact that the earth goes round the sun. He may be prepared to give weight to the boy's actions and merits, but not to his complexes. So here too the emphasis is upon the importance of the conceptual mechanism, the tools, the spectacles through which we view the facts. A general injunction to consider the facts does not seem to add up to much more than a warning against intolerance, or against being cocksure in one's moral judgements: a warning which is always useful, but does not carry one very far.

Moreover, in one important way the two components of 'being reasonable' are interdependent. It is the actual discovery of facts, and the drawing of people's attention to them, which itself changes our use of conceptual tools. Thus, most schoolmasters would today take courses (*b*) or (*c*), the more humanitarian courses: whereas in previous eras course (*a*), the course of strict justice, would have been more popular. This is not, I think, primarily because philosophers have recently shed very much new light on justice as a concept: would that they had! It is rather because much more attention is paid to people in general, and boys in particular, in respect of their being sensitive, having feelings, suffering serious damage by over-rough treatment, and so on: because the psychological or clinical approach to people has gained ground. If the concept of justice is less used than it was, it is not because its logic now seems to most people deficient in the context of problems of this kind. Rather it is perishing by the wayside, losing its power by default. To say that philosophers have no business with the empirical facts, therefore, is in one important respect misleading. Certainly the philosopher's business is not to discover empirical facts. But it is his business to see where the discovery of facts bears upon our conceptual tools, and to imagine cases where such discovery might bear even more heavily than it does already. Thus books like Huxley's *Brave New World* and Orwell's *1984* obviously contain important features for the moral and political philosopher, in whatever sense we use the word 'philosopher'; and the works of advanced science fiction writers, by presenting him with empirical conditions very unlike our own, should stimulate clarity in much the same way as the invention of examples, borderline cases, extreme cases and so forth helps to elucidate the logic of our thought.

Basically the failure of modern philosophy to throw off its sterility and dryness is due to its failure to give full weight to the concept of 'being reasonable'. Most modern analytic philosophers give the impression of being liberal, tolerant, agnostic, slightly left-wing, and rather tender-minded. On their lips the phrase 'being reasonable' suggests a gentlemanly lack of unwarranted aggression or dogmatism, and a desire not to cause trouble. It is rather like the concept of 'the reasonable man' in law: and it suffers from the usual liberal failing of being insufficiently tough-minded and radical to satisfy anyone except other liberals. Usage of this kind arouses people like D. H. Lawrence to reject reason in favour of the 'dark, nameless forces' deep down in the human personality; for whenever reason is not extended to cover enough ground people will always use something else to cover the rest of it—faith, or instinct, or dark, nameless forces.

The trouble with the 'reasonable' man in law, or the 'good' man whom Lawrence shoots at, is that the criteria for these words have become too hardened. A 'reasonable' man in Calvin's Geneva would have testified to the effect that the sight of female ankles was shocking, and a 'good' Victorian might have thought that poor people should not have medical attention if they did not deserve it. Philosophers must keep the game more open than this: not by being personally rebellious in society, but by being conceptually rebellious, by continually calling into question our conceptual tools and the criteria for our moral language rather than by seeking merely to expound them. Without this, the impression is bound to be given that everything is really all right. One would like to be able to say that Lawrence was (in this respect anyway) more reasonable than his opponents, because he drew attention to important features which should be taken into account in moral problems. But it sounds queer to say this, because of restrictions on the word 'reasonable'.

This chapter is meant to be inconclusive, is meant to say only that there is more to be said, more to be done, than most modern moral philosophy seems to imply. What follows is an attempt to say and do some of it. The attempt will be a fumbling one, because we seem to have got to the stage where slickness and neatness will carry us no further. We just have to grope around: the reader will have to wait for anything that looks like a reform programme.

CHAPTER II

THE PURPOSES OF MORAL LANGUAGE

I F philosophy can really help people to think and act more reasonably in moral contexts, as I suggested in the last chapter, then it can only do so by increasing our clarity and removing our misunderstanding. It is plain that we are liable to any amount of confusion and misunderstanding about all the various moral questions and decisions which constantly confront us: so that, from this point of view, philosophy has the never-ending task of patiently clarifying each particular piece of confusion as it arises. But there is, I believe, one particular piece of misunderstanding which is connected with the nature of morality itself, and with our own attitude to it. My object in this chapter is to clear up this confusion, because such clarification is an essential preliminary to any acceptable methodology of ethics.

I. TWO TYPES OF MORAL THINKING

A brief consideration of our own feelings, of what passes in our minds before reaching a decision on moral issues, will remind us of two kinds of experience which seem to us to be basically different. The first is our experience of duty, conscience, obligation, or some kind of moral imperative. What terms can be best used to describe this experience is not immediately important here. It is sufficient that the experience can be identified. It appears to us as some sort of external command or demand, arising from some source which carries the emotional weight of authority: it may (though it need not) be connected with religion, and have the force of a divine command: or it may be not very far removed from the simple fear of punishment or social disapproval. The second is our experience of our own feelings and desires in so far as they are not dictated by external imperatives. These exercise force upon us, but their pressure is internal and does not present itself to us as authoritative. Thus we may feel sympathetic, loving, lustful, angry, greedy, lazy, and so on: such feelings ask for satisfaction in a sense, but do not demand it with the weight of authority.[1]

We may next observe how this difference appears in ordinary moral discussions on a non-philosophical level. Questions like 'Ought a starving beggar to steal a loaf of bread?', 'Should I keep my promise, even though it may bring suffering to many people?', 'If I were to press a button and kill one unknown Chinese baby, but acquire £1,000,000 to spend on charity, would I be justified?', all suggest a conflict between the external pressures of moral authority (the rules against stealing, breaking promises, and committing murder) and the internal pressures of desire or sentiment (the desire to feed the hungry, to minimise suffering, and to help others). For many unsophisticated people, indeed, such discussions sometimes amount to little more than an imaginary battle-ground, on which the two sorts of pressure conflict and the victory goes to the stronger. The question 'What should I do?' becomes assimilated to the question 'What *would* I do?': the stronger pressure is regarded as decisive for both questions.

Finally, we are also familiar with this difference in more general terms. At the practical level we contrast

---

[1] We could obviously use the language of psychoanalysis to differentiate between these two types of experiences: we can say that the former spring from the super-ego, and the latter from the id.

duty with expediency, ideals with 'practical politics', the moral law with worldly wisdom or conscience with common sense: and we may debate these general issues as well as the more particular questions mentioned above. At the philosophical level we may talk of intuitionism and utilitarianism, deontological and teleological ethics, morality of motive and morality of consequence, or Gesinnungsethik and Erfolgsethik.[1] It will be convenient for our purpose to give titles of a more general kind to either side in this distinction: and for the sake of simplicity I shall use the term Moralism for the first side, and the term Factualism for the second.[2]

Since Moralism and Factualism operate in a great many fields, and on a great many levels of human thought, feeling and action, we could discuss the differences between them in a great many ways. We could consider them in terms of individual psychology, in terms of sociological function, in purely linguistic terms, or in a wider philosophical context. Since these fields are different and yet closely connected, it would be misleading at this stage to offer any single criterion; for a distinction as broad and general as this one is unlikely to fall within the scope of a single criterion. Here it is better to be inconclusive than to oversimplify. We can

---

[1] I have followed Professor D. M. Mackinnon's use of these two terms and in general owe a great deal to his work *A Study of Ethical Theory* (A. and C. Black, 1957).

[2] I have preferred to coin these two terms, rather than to use terms which already have philosophical currency (e.g. 'deontological' and 'teleological'), for three reasons: first, because they are more likely to make sense to the general reader; secondly, because I am concerned with more than just philosophical thought—the distinction is not one of theoretical ethics alone; thirdly, because I am not by any means certain that the distinction marked by (say) 'deontological' and 'teleological' is the same, even on a theoretical level, as the rather broader and less tidy distinction which I wish to make.

best begin, therefore, by noting some instances where the difference between these two types of ethical thinking seems plain.

(1) First, a difference which suggests that the terms Moralism and Factualism are not too inapposite. Moralists and Factualists seem to defend their beliefs in different ways. Suppose we are discussing divorce by consent, or sexual promiscuity. If a Moralist were opposed to these practices, and asked to defend his opinion, he would say something like 'Any decent man knows in his heart that promiscuity is wrong', or 'Divorce is against the will of God', or 'Your conscience tells you that you mustn't commit adultery'. A Factualist would perhaps say 'Easy divorce does harm to the children', or 'Without sexual morality we should have social chaos'. The Moralist defends his view, not by reference to facts or social results, but by reference to a moral code, or conscience, or religion— all things which are not 'facts' in the same sense that a rise in the illegitimate birth-rate is a fact. The Factualist, by contrast, looks for facts and social results, and has no time for a morality that is not closely bound up with them.

(2) Now consider a more general difference. The Moralist will defend morality as a whole (as opposed to particular moral opinions) simply because it *is* morality, not because its constituent parts fulfil any particular purpose. The moral law, some Moralists would say, is a real law which can be known: it presents itself to us as an imperative: it is written in God's commandments or our own consciences. It is not just a convenience. But the Factualist regards moral rules in much the same light as other rules—that is, as useful guides towards achieving certain ends: ultimately they are just a convenience. They have no particular validity in themselves, no absolute

39

authority. If they serve human ends, they are good rules: if they do not, they can be scrapped. To put it briefly: the Moralist thinks you ought to do what is right because it *is* right, whereas the Factualist thinks you ought to do what is right because it is constructive or brings about a good result. Hence the Moralist will talk in terms of duty or obligation: the Factualist will talk about ends and means, the promotion of human happiness, and so on.

(3) In judging human behaviour, the Moralist will concentrate on a man's intentions, on his choices, on whether he exercised free will, and on those parts of his personality which (in his view) are alone morally relevant. The Factualist will not make such a sharp division: to him, it might sometimes be just as bad to be stupid as to intend to kill somebody. He will not necessarily grant any unique importance or status to moral intentions or choices. Thus the Moralist will be interested in questions like 'What did he intend to do?' or 'Did he try to do so-and-so?'—questions that a judge might ask the jury to consider in a lawsuit: whereas the Factualist will consider a man's motives as distinct from his intentions, and ask 'What made him do that?' or 'What were the causes of his action?'—questions appropriate to a psychologist rather than a judge. The Moralist tries to get in a position where he can say 'Guilty' or 'Not guilty': the Factualist tries to explain, and to give an overall assessment of a man's character.

We may generalise these differences in all sorts of ways: but perhaps the most illuminating is to say that the Moralist approaches human thoughts, intentions and behaviour with an eye on their relations to some external authority, whereas the Factualist approaches them with an eye on their relations to human nature and the nature of human society. Hence the Moralist is not primarily concerned to adopt a critical approach to any particular piece of morality, or to morality as a whole, because his chief interest lies in our endeavour to live up to that morality: the morality itself can, for this purpose, be taken for granted. The Factualist will be primarily concerned to study the facts of human nature, and thence to build up a morality which in some sense fits those facts. Again, since the Moralist's concern is with man *vis-à-vis* the rules of external authority, he is chiefly interested in those parts of man which reflect man's response, or lack of response, to that authority: basically he is concerned with how *loyal* a person is to authority. The Factualist, to whom human nature rather than authority is primary, is basically concerned not with loyalty but with satisfaction, with the proper development and employment of human nature.

This is, of course, a difference of approach rather than a difference of belief, and the Moralist and Factualist may have other things in common for which this distinction is not intended to cater. Thus, both Moralist and Factualist no doubt have 'ultimate values', which cannot be proved in the way that empirical propositions can be proved: such ultimate criteria as 'pleasure' or 'what makes for human happiness' are in much the same logical boat as such ultimate criteria as 'the will of God' or 'what satisfies the human conscience'. Further, it is not always true that the Moralist will support actually established authorities and that the Factualist will always be critical of them. A Moralist may be in a minority in his society (as a conscientious objector, for instance); but he is still a Moralist in so far as he is concerned with the acceptance of authority—only it is not the authority of the state, but of some moral law (a law against any kind of killing, perhaps) which he considers more authoritative. Similarly the Factualist may very likely accept the moral and social rules and authority operative in his society: though he would still be a Factualist if he accepted these rules, not simply because they were authoritative, but because he thought they fitted human nature. Again, the Moralist need not necessarily be more 'moralistic' in the popular sense than the Factualist: that is, he need not necessarily act in a more authoritarian manner, or be more anxious to impose his principles on others. The Factualist need not be any less violent in his beliefs just because they are founded on human nature.

Indeed, there is plainly a sense in which the Factualist as well as the Moralist insists on authority: that is, he insists on the authority of the facts. But there is a difference in the sort of thing that authorises the beliefs of either: a difference in the provenance of the authority. For the Moralist the authority is external: it may be the rules of a particular society, a set of basic moral principles like the Ten Commandments, the dictates of conscience, the divine will, and so on. For the Factualist the 'authority'—and it is really only by a kind of metaphor that we can use the word here—is an internal one: the authority of fact. The Moralist regards human beings as under some sort of control, the control of law: the Factualist regards them as following some sort of guidance, the guidance of nature.

There is no doubt that for most people, in the course of their everyday lives, the contrast between Moralism and Factualism seems to take the form of a conflict. In moral debate, whether with ourselves or with other people, the two approaches seem contradictory. Each seems to make different and often conflicting demands upon us, and we do not know to which we ought to attend. The situation is in many respects analogous to religious debate or doubt, in which the respective demands of Faith and Reason similarly conflict, or seem to conflict. It is almost as if two voices spoke to us, we might say the voices of Conscience and Expediency, or perhaps Justice and Mercy, or perhaps Law and Desire. If such a picture seems naïve, it is at least not very far removed from the psychoanalysts' description of what happens when people face moral situations. Moreover, people are very fond of this picture: we like to contrast different points of view under title-headings, such as 'Arts *v.* Science', or 'Masculine and Feminine', or 'The Older Generation and Modern Young People'. Nor is there any question that the conflict is real, in the sense that people really feel the tugs and pulls of these points of view, even if they do not actually hear voices.

Nevertheless, the philosopher does well to become suspicious of such a picture. The conflict may be unreal in the sense that it is not logically necessary: and there is hope that, once it is seen to be logically unnecessary, it may become avoidable in practice. Thus, one person may say of a table that it is a piece of wood with four legs, and another that it is a compound of atoms and void: and there is no conflict here, though we can see how there might be one if someone were to say fiercely 'But *really* it's only atoms and void', with the implied denial that it is really a piece of wood with four legs. Or again, one person may say that a cathedral is stone and mortar, and another that it is a work of art: and here too a conflict seems silly, though we can see how it might arise—if, say, there were a question of dismantling the cathedral to build houses for working men, or clearing the space to make a children's playground. We would say in such cases 'It depends from what point of view you consider it', or (more acutely) 'It depends what purposes you have in mind'.

We can only clear up this apparent conflict by a consideration of the metaphysics which lie behind Moralism and Factualism. Each has an implicit metaphysic which it uses, though perhaps clumsily, to defend its own part in the conflict: the Moralist's metaphysic being designed to support his insistence on man's response to external authority, and the Factualist's to support his insistence on the facts of human nature. It is important to see that the Moralist's metaphysic, in particular, must rely not so much upon the objective validity of some particular authority or set of moral principles, as upon a picture of human beings which will enable him to regard them as responsible and responsive to authority. Thus, human beings must be morally free, capable of virtue and vice, deserving of praise and blame, able to do right or wrong, and in general morally responsible—in a different sense of 'responsible' from that in which we say, for instance, that the wind was responsible for blowing down the chimney-pot. In their relations to authority men must be capable of being judged, assessed as guilty or innocent, and justly punished or rewarded. All these concepts, as they are used by the Moralist, relate to authority: and they all seem tacitly to support a metaphysical picture of human beings which is not necessarily a true picture. The Factualist metaphysic, on the other hand, need not grind any such axe. For him, all that need matter is that human nature can be investigated: that the facts can be discovered. Factualism implies that human beings are explainable, predictable, and capable of being analysed, and can in

44

principle be unrolled on the table like a blue-print, in order that we may study them and see what ought to be done with them. The Moralist reacts very sharply to any such idea. A typical reaction is that of a clergyman who gave the University Sermon at Oxford University, and complained about the psychiatric or clinical approach to homosexuals and criminals on the grounds that such an approach treats men 'as if they were machines'.

2. MEN AND MACHINES

It is only recently that the advance of science—not only of the discoveries of science, that is, but the prestige of science—has reached a point when many people are prepared to say more or less flatly 'Men are like machines', or even 'Men are machines'. No doubt many factors have contributed to this situation: progress in cybernetics and the widespread acceptance of a psychological approach to human beings are not the least. For the first time many people are seriously in doubt, for instance, about the correct method of approach to criminals: some are prepared to forgo a moralistic approach and adopt a purely clinical one, and almost everybody feels the tugs of the two viewpoints very strongly. Challenging propositions, of the kind that often herald a reorientation of categories and concepts, are put forward, such as 'All criminals are insane', or 'You can't ever blame anybody, really'. Even the most convinced Moralist has to pay lip-service to psychology, and for a defence of his views tends to resort to severely practical arguments: if we adopted a purely clinical approach we could not have a legal system, school-boys would do no work, immorality would increase, and so forth. This kind of recrudescent utilitarianism is more difficult to shrug off in the twentieth century than in the nineteenth: chiefly because it is less naïve. It is no longer bound up with ideas which now seem quaint and unsophisticated, such as *laissez-faire* and a hedonistic calculus; on the contrary, it is backed by a depth psychology which makes full allowances, and may even be thought to give full explanations, for all the phenomena which used to be the standard ammunition of the Moralist: the existence of conscience, guilt, desire for punishment, belief in absolute morality, religion, the tragedy of the human situation (itself a Freudian phrase)—even original sin.

'Men are like machines' is a blunt and challenging way of expressing the belief that human beings are amenable to scientific study. What sort of claim is this? It is not, of course, suggested that human beings have cogs and levers: nothing is gained against the claim by pointing out that the more we learn about human beings, the less they look like watches or clockwork trains—just as no point is gained against science as a whole by showing that Newton's cosmology is less efficient than Einstein's. Nor is it suggested that human beings, like machines, are made for a particular purpose: still less that they cannot choose, suffer, feel emotion, act originally, create works of art, and so forth. If the definition of 'machine' is made to exclude such aptitudes, of course, then it is obviously but trivially true that human beings are not like machines, or not like any machines which we know today. The claim is rather that human beings are in one particular and important *logical* way like machines: that they work by cause and effect. This looks like some sort of creed or working principle: 'Everything works by cause and effect', a sort of scientist's slogan or statement of faith, rather like (or perhaps identical with) a belief in the 'uniformity of nature'. But we are familiar with the way in which scientists are continually

46

being saddled with metaphysical beliefs of this kind: religious writers reiterate that science continually makes assumptions of faith. In order to work at all, it is alleged, scientists have to believe in the omnipresence of 'laws of nature', in the existence of a planned or designed world, in the validity of induction (so that the future can be like the past), and so forth. But the fact is that scientists go on working quite happily without making any such acts of faith at all, either consciously or unconsciously.

This is not at all odd, since it is not necessary to say 'Everything works by cause and effect' and mean it as a creed. The Moralist, the religious believer, and the critic of modern analytic philosophy all tend to seize avidly upon propositions which do, admittedly, often have the air of dogma, with the intention of showing that they are merely other dogmas different from their own but of the same logical status.[1] There may have been scientists who propounded the belief in cause and effect with the air of those setting up against other dogmas—the dogmas of religion, for instance: indeed, some scientists (whether opposed to religion or in favour of it) are over-fond of giving their science a top dressing of metaphysics. But it is hardly fair to take them seriously.

Few people, I imagine, would wish to object to the cause-and-effect thesis (whatever its logical status) if it were not applied to people. That the rest of the universe works by cause and effect, and is amenable to scientific investigation, is today entirely tolerable to the most ardent Moralists. In the rest of the universe, we all say

[1] Thus it is a favourite trick of some philosophers to treat the verification principle as a dogma, and then render it innocuous by pointing out that it is itself unverifiable. In fact the principle is best understood as an observation about language and thought, not as a dogma at all: however false an impression may have been created by its early proponents.

nowadays, things do not 'just happen': there has to be a reason, an explanation. However, this is something comparatively new in human history, almost as new as the extreme view that human beings are like machines. It is not so many centuries ago that we used to regard physical objects in the light of people, or personal entities with wills and desires. In pre-classical Greece we find the view that the Fates chase the sun back to its proper course if it is wicked enough to go off the rails; primitive tribes blame and punish the spear which shed blood; and in general (as the Frankforts put it briefly) 'natural phenomena were regularly conceived in terms of human experience' before the rise of science.[1] It would be otiose to go into this more fully. Now, the situation is reversed: we are beginning to conceive human experience in terms borrowed from natural phenomena, or indeed to conceive human beings *as* natural phenomena. Basically, the objection of the Moralist to Freudian and other depth psychology is not that its theories about causation in human beings are wrong: it is that we have no business to theorise in this way at all. It was not that Freud was mistaken in the causes he suggested: it was that he set up to suggest causes at all.

It still seems to the average person much more plausible to object to the cause-and-effect thesis when it comes to people. Everyone nowadays is prepared to take questions of natural science seriously. 'Why do things fall downwards?': to say 'They just do' seems to us simply not good enough. But 'Why did he do that?': to say 'He just did', or 'He just wanted to', seems perfectly adequate. It takes quite an effort to believe with Freud, even after several decades, that slips of the tongue must be taken seriously—

[1] H. and H. A. Frankfort, *Before Philosophy* (Pelican edition, 1949), p. 12.

that there is a cause for their occurrence. If you press someone about the behaviour of people, and ask 'But *why* did he make that slip?' or 'There must have been *some* reason for his choosing that' or 'Yes, but *why* did he hate his wife?', you get an impatient frown: apparently you have asked a silly question. We know that the greatness of scientists consists precisely in taking seriously questions which had never been seriously asked, in regarding common phenomena as things requiring explanation. But with the choices of men we find this difficult to swallow. I make some trivial and spontaneous choice, like touching my right knee when I might have touched my left: and a serious scientist buttonholes me with the question ' *Why* did you touch your *right* knee, h'm?' It takes a lot to answer calmly 'Well, I really don't know, but I suppose there must have been a cause'.[1]

Anyway (we feel), why *must* there have been a cause of the kind here demanded? Why should it not 'just happen'? We can always say that an event or phenomenon was 'pure chance': that it was in principle inexplicable and unpredictable: that it 'had no cause': that it 'just happened'. Moreover, we can say this seriously. We are often accustomed to say casually of any odd occurrence that it was not in the common run of events, while being prepared to give way when pressed with the question 'Surely you don't mean there really is *no* explanation *at all*?': but if we like, we need not give way. But then we must face the consequences. To cling seriously to this position involves more than the belief that the phenomenon

---

[1] It is, of course, often possible to give a *reason* which is not a *cause*, in the scientific sense, for some action. (Thus we could say 'He chose to do that in order to help his friend', or 'He wrote down 12 because he was asked what twice six is, and twice six *is* twelve'.) But this is not in question here: we are concerned only with the demand for a scientific cause.

is very odd or unusual, or that science will have a very hard job to make sense of it, or even that science will require new types of evidence and new theories to make sense of it (in the way, for instance, that the evidence and theorisation required for microscopic physics or the social sciences differ from those required for Newtonian physics). The position involves the belief that the phenomenon is in principle inexplicable.

To what extent is it rational to believe this? There are obviously overwhelming arguments against it. To say seriously 'It just happened' is in effect to say 'We shall never—can never—explain it': and this is rash, since phenomena of all kinds have steadily yielded to explanation. Science has, in fact, advanced: and to believe that any particular phenomenon will forever defeat it is simply to make an unwise bet. Scientists do not *have* to believe that science will always be successful (perhaps this is belief in the 'uniformity of nature'?): they can simply argue from the fact that it has been successful in the past to the high probability that it will be successful in the future—and this, for all the so-called 'problem of induction', is the very archetype of rational belief. Or else we can say that it seems more expedient to assume the possibility of explanation, quite irrespective of its probability: it would be useful to explain the phenomenon, so that it seems merely silly to deny ourselves the chance by saying it is in principle inexplicable. Indeed, the more one considers this matter the more it looks as if, by refusing to entertain the possibility of explanation, we are simply applying the axe of dogma and prejudice: like savages, for instance, whose objection to scientific investigation of their religious tenets is chiefly motivated by a desire to retain their mystery. Such motivation, moreover, is plainly not absent from those who object to regarding men as machines. The psychological train of thought runs: 'Scientific investigation means a lessening of the mystery of human personality, which means the devaluation of things like human rights and dignity, which means chaos.'

But perhaps the belief is not intended to be logically like this at all. If a possibility—in this case, the possibility of explanation—is being denied, two things may be intended. We may mean that it is empirically or practically impossible: thus, I may say that it is impossible for me to swim the Atlantic or suddenly to become 12 feet high. But if we mean this, we are always prepared to retreat under pressure. Somebody says 'After all, you *might* suddenly develop fantastic powers of swimming, or suddenly eat something which makes you 12 feet high, mightn't you?': and we say 'Well, yes, I suppose I *might*, but it's very unlikely'. This is not to admit that we should have said 'very unlikely' instead of 'impossible', for there is a perfectly good sense of 'impossible' which emerges simply as 'very unlikely in practice' when judged by the strictest standards. In other words, it is possible to conceive of a situation in which I could swim the Atlantic or grow 12 feet high: it is not logical nonsense to say that I could do these things. It is simply that I would place a very heavy bet against its ever happening. As we have seen, to place such a bet on the ultimate inexplicability of some phenomenon seems unwise. But we may mean, alternatively, that there is no logical possibility of explanation: thus, I may say that it is impossible for a triangle to have four sides, or (though more questionably) that it is impossible for an object to be in two places at the same time. To defend this, I should have to show that there was something about the meaning (or the grammar, as

Wittgenstein puts it) of 'triangle' which logically excluded a triangle having four sides, and something about the meaning of 'object' which logically excluded an object being in two places at the same time. The belief in explicability may be of this kind.

To take a case which is not only parallel to this but importantly connected with it, we may mean by 'miracle' something which human beings will in practice never be able to explain (because it is too hard for them, as it were): or we may mean something which logically cannot be explained, which is by definition inexplicable. Believers in the ultimate inexplicability of human beings face a similar ambiguity. The motives for uncertainty are plain enough, since if they stick to the first sense, miracles become devalued: they are no more than phenomena which are very, very difficult to understand. They may be 'mysterious' in this sense, but in no other important sense. For we can, of course, conceive of circumstances which would enable us to understand a miracle or a human action: and without much difficulty, either. This first sense being inadequate for defending whatever it is that they wish to defend, therefore, they shift to the second sense, the sense in which miracles are by definition inexplicable. But this too is unsatisfactory. First, we are now beginning to play what looks like a pointless linguistic game with our own rules: we defend the mystery of miracles only by pre-empting the word 'miracle'. We cease saying anything about the real world. Our opponents now deny that there are miracles at all in this pre-empted sense, so that we have gained nothing. Secondly, we have now made 'miracles' into something of which no sense can, logically or conceivably, be made: and is this what we really want? Surely not: surely religious believers, for instance, would want to say that there *is* sense in miracles but that human beings cannot grasp it: that God *has* purposes but that human beings cannot understand them: that he moves in a mysterious way, but that this way is not purely haphazard.

A belief that human beings, or indeed any phenomena, are by definition inexplicable, therefore, will not do. For nobody is going to pretend that there is something about the meaning and grammar of 'human being', or 'human choice', or 'event', or 'phenomenon', which logically involves inexplicability: and even if somebody had the nerve to pre-empt any of these words so that they did logically involve inexplicability, which is unlikely, it would profit him nothing. Yet to retire to the first sense of 'impossible', by which it is asserted that it is empirically impossible to explain human beings, seems equally unreasonable. The dilemma of this dichotomy is inescapable.

To abandon our opposition to the view, however, seems to entail consequences which are little short of revolutionary. Indeed, the Moralist might suppose that it entails abandoning morality altogether. Morality does not apply to machines. At the very least there is a whole host of concepts which form the corpus of moral thinking, and which when applied to machines look merely silly. The notions of moral freedom, of justice, virtue and vice, reward and punishment, praise and blame, guilt and innocence, together with subordinate concepts such as loyalty, honesty, purity, self-sacrifice and so forth, all seem quite inapplicable. Then there are words which would only apply in what to a Moralist would seem a devalued sense: thus, we can talk about a machine going 'right' or 'wrong', or being 'good' or 'bad', or we can say 'it was the "fault" of the sparking-plugs', or 'the fly-wheel was "responsible"', but the words here lack the moral overtones which they have when applied to human beings and human actions. Again, all talk about motives seems absurd, and concepts like 'will-power', 'trying hard' and even the 'self' become irrelevant. Religious words like 'soul' or 'spirit', 'salvation', 'grace' and so forth seem sillier still. All this is very frightening.

A Moralist might try to settle the issue quickly by saying that if men are machines, no meaning can be attached to moral concepts: and that since morality and moral concepts do have meaning, men cannot be machines. Thus if men are machines, they cannot have intentions, since machines do not have intentions, but only motive forces: and since human beings plainly do have intentions, they are not machines. A similar argument would apply in the case of concepts like 'trying', or 'free will'. But this argument is not conclusive. The Factualist could hardly deny that these concepts make sense of a sort, but would claim that their meaning is fogged by the Moralists' picture of what human beings are like. 'No doubt these concepts stand for *something*,' he would say, 'but they will stand for things which work by cause and effect, not for curious metaphysical-Moralist entities. No doubt human beings have intentions, and machines do not: but this is simply to say that human beings have bits of mechanism in them which machines do not have. One could in principle predict when a man would try or intend to do something. So the picture of man as a very complex machine can still stand.' To the Factualist, words like 'intentions', 'determination', 'will-power', etc. are just inevitably clumsy descriptions of parts of the human personality about which we know little, and which we therefore cannot describe precisely or scientifically. He would suggest that as psychology advances such words would gradually be replaced by other words which are firmly established in psychological theory: in the same way, perhaps, as words like 'super-ego' and 'id' are beginning to take over from words like 'guilt' and 'desire'.

It is important to realise that if the logic of the men-as-machines view is valid at all, it is valid for all features of human personality. For there is a standing temptation to single out one or more such features, and make it look as if they are somehow exempt from causality or immune to scientific prediction and explanation. Thus for a long time now the phrase 'free will' has seemed to many people to describe some feature of human personality which is, perhaps by definition, immune from causality—we might say, not a part of the machine at all. It is interesting to see how closely this corresponds with more modern views. Hampshire, for instance, singles out the notion of 'trying' as offering some hope of escape from causal prediction, or some special kind of moral freedom, and writes 'It must (logically) always be possible to try'.[1] But if 'trying' (like 'free will') is supposed to describe some empirically verifiable piece of human behaviour, or feature of human personality, then it must be logically possible that this behaviour or feature should at times be absent—and that it will necessarily be absent when the conditions that cause or sustain it are absent. (Thus it seems much more natural to say that there are times when people cannot try to do things: for instance, when they are asleep, or under the influence of drugs or hypnosis.) Certainly concepts like 'free will', 'trying', 'intending' and others may stand for features which we like to regard as of central importance to human beings

[1] Stuart Hampshire, *Thought and Action* (Chatto and Windus, 1959), p. 189.

as moral agents—as a sort of inner nucleus of human personality, so to speak. But these features are still part of the machine.

3. COMMON CONCEPTS IN MORALISM

So far we have not done much more than make the Moralist look silly, at least in so far as we have supposed him to challenge the view which has been bluntly expressed by the assertion 'Men are like machines'. I should like, however, to delay the business of doing justice to the Moralist (both as regards his moral feelings and his moral language) till a much later stage: for it is essential at this point to expand the consequences of this assertion, which we have seen to be a reasonable one. We can note, however, that though men may be like machines, they may also be like other things. The view of men as machines is not an exclusive view: indeed, the whole point of such a striking parallel seems designed to press one particular approach to human beings upon us, to establish it as valid and noteworthy, without necessarily excluding other views. I shall take it that to fight against this view is a mistake on the part of the Moralist.

Yet even so it would be a mistake to ride roughshod over the concepts of Moralism. It will be wiser to single out some concepts which are central to Moralism, and try to assess them on their own. Four such concepts in particular call for discussion. First, there is the concept of freedom or free will, which seems of all moral concepts the most directly and immediately threatened by the men-as-machines view. Secondly, there is the overall concept of morality. Thirdly, there is the concept of subordinate moral principles (honesty, truthfulness, etc.). Fourthly, there is the concept of justice, together with the cognate concepts of reward and punishment, which has always been a rock against which Factualism has dashed itself in vain. All these concepts are deeply engrained into our moral thinking, and it seems both unfair and unwise to suppose that the men-as-machines view has totally obliterated and nullified them, as it were by shock tactics. The Moralist would certainly hold that they were logically inconsistent with the Factualist view: perhaps even that, on any kind of utilitarian or men-as-machines thesis, they were incomprehensible. If this thesis reduces the concepts to logical nonsense, then it also reduces itself to absurdity. I think it is important to show that this is not the case: that the concepts can be shown to make sense without prejudice to the machine thesis. It may not be the sort of sense the Moralist wants to make. But we can safely leave the task of doing justice to his sort of sense till later.

(a) *Freedom and Compulsion*

The problem of freedom or free will consists of finding valid criteria for our application of certain common words and our use of well-known concepts, which we apply to human behaviour and actions. Under certain conditions, it seems, we describe men as 'acting freely', as 'guilty', 'blameworthy', or 'wicked', and as 'deserving punishment'; under other conditions we describe them as 'forced' or 'compelled', 'not to blame', 'not responsible' or 'acting involuntarily'. It is this group of concepts to which we refer when we use phrases like 'It's not his fault', 'I did it against my will', 'He's to be pitied rather than blamed', and so on. In other words, we make a distinction between free action and compulsive action: between acting of one's own free will, and acting under compulsion. It is the basis of this distinction which is commonly called into question.

Let us first be clear that this is not a distinction between freedom and predictability. I doubt whether any such distinction has been made in practice, except by muddle-headed philosophers. Ordinary men do not behave, and do not talk, as if the predictability of their actions disqualified them from being free. I can predict that a child will work out a simple sum correctly, or that he will not stab me with a carving-knife; but unless someone is threatening him with dire punishment if he gets the sum wrong or does stab me, no compulsion is being exercised on the child. On the contrary, 'unpredictable' is if anything a word of dispraise; whereas freedom is something which we cherish, so that it would be very queer indeed if freedom were to depend upon unpredictability.

But it is a mistake to suppose that after having explained, as some philosophers have very adequately explained,[1] this particular muddle, we are left with nothing that can properly be called a problem. There is indeed no particular difficulty in appreciating and setting out the criteria which, in everyday life, we actually employ in distinguishing between free and compulsive actions. We all know, for instance, the difference between jumping and being pushed, between stealing and kleptomania, between signing a contract freely and signing it under duress. We all know when we would accept evidence for the truth of statements like 'He could have acted otherwise', or 'He could have chosen differently': these are part of normal reasoning.[2] All this is to say that in everyday life,

---

[1] E.g. Professor Ayer in 'Freedom and Necessity', *Polemic*, no. 5, 1946 (reprinted in his *Philosophical Essays*).

[2] Cf. Nowell-Smith, *Ethics*, pp. 276–7.

as in the law-courts, we have an adequate working definition of what counts as freedom or compulsion, sanity or insanity, responsibility or constraint. But there is still felt to be a problem of some kind. The situation generates worry and gives rise to anxiety.

This anxiety usually expresses itself in such questions as 'How can we know whether our criteria for freedom and compulsion are really the right ones?', 'How can we be quite sure that those whom we now regard as responsible and blameworthy are not really suffering from an unknown compulsion?', or more generally, 'Can we set up criteria for free and compelled action that will be permanently valid?' These questions are legitimate; for it is a fact that our criteria fluctuate. The impression is often given that the more psychologists discover about our behaviour the more we are found to be acting under compulsion; and thus we tend to imagine that the circle of our freedom is forever diminishing as psychology advances. Thus Hampshire writes: '...as our psychological and physiological knowledge of human actions and reactions increases, the range of human actions of which we can reasonably say "an alternative action was possible", or "he could have acted otherwise", necessarily diminishes.'[1] If this impression is a true one—and it has yet to be shown to be false—then our anxiety is quite genuine. For if a man could not have acted otherwise, it seems sense to say that he was compelled to act as he did; and though we cannot be sure that psychological knowledge will enable us to explain all our actions, there is equally no guarantee that it will not. In any case, we should not be satisfied with a circle of freedom which is rapidly shrinking to an unknown size.

[1] Stuart Hampshire, *Spinoza* (Pelican edition, 1951), p. 151.

Let us consider why it is that this circle seems to us to be shrinking. Our working distinction between free and compelled action, correctly analysed by Aristotle,[1] is not difficult to apprehend. Free action occurs when the 'cause' or 'origin' of the action is 'within' the agent: compelled action occurs when it is 'outside' the agent. The question, therefore, resolves itself into the question of what is to count as an 'outside' cause, and what is to count as 'inside' cause. Under normal circumstances, we usually know the answer to this question. Being pushed, threatened, or diseased are all cases of the operation of 'outside' causes; whereas wanting or desiring to do something, or choosing or deciding to do it, are 'inside' causes. What is disturbing about new psychological knowledge is that it seems to suggest that a great many causes which we had previously classified as 'inside', and therefore not compulsive, are really 'outside', and therefore compulsive. Kleptomania and compulsion neuroses are examples of this kind; but perhaps the best, because the most disturbing, example is of a man who acts as the result of a hypnotic suggestion of which everyone except the hypnotist is ignorant. For example, a hypnotist may suggest to someone that in an hour's time he will take off his coat and open all the windows in the room; and the man will do this even if in doing so he suffers severely from the cold. He will invent reasons for his action, and even— this is the disturbing point—imagine himself to be acting freely. Yet when we found out that his action was due to the hypnotist's command, we should have no hesitation in calling it compulsive.

Many people feel that all their actions may be compulsive in this way: that is, the result of 'outside' causes of which

[1] Aristotle, *Nicomachean Ethics*, III, i, 10 and 20.

they are ignorant. For it is not necessary that the compulsion should come from a person, as from the hypnotist: other things can compel besides people, including factors which are commonly described under the general categories of 'heredity' and 'environment'. Compulsion is not necessarily consciously directed: this is a point which enthusiastic advocates of political freedom tend to overlook. Nor are the most overt forms of compulsion necessarily the most compulsive: indoctrination at a subconscious level may be more effective than physical force or threats. All these considerations provide us with legitimate grounds for worry. For though at any one time we might be able to draw up a list of compulsive or 'outside' causes which we have discovered, and though we might be able on this basis to establish a distinction between free and compelled action which we could use in our moral and legal judgements, we cannot be sure that this list will be exhaustive, or that our criteria for the distinction can ever be more than temporary.

To put the problem in a slightly different way: It does not seem satisfactory, as a criterion of freedom, to say 'Any action shall at any time count as free, unless we have good reason to believe that it results from compulsive causes'. For the fact that we do not have good reason to believe this may, it appears, often be due merely to our psychological ignorance. Until we discovered kleptomania, we had no good reason to believe that any cases of stealing were compulsive; and until we found out that the man took off his coat and opened the window owing to a post-hypnotic command, we naturally thought that he was acting freely. In both cases, we were genuinely mistaken. In order to avoid similar mistakes, it seems as if we shall at least have to confess to ignorance of whether any action is free, unless we already know that it is due to compulsion. And once we have discovered a compulsive cause for an action, this by definition excludes the action from any possible class of free actions.

There is, however, something queer about the way in which this anxiety has arisen. We know that to have discovered a cause is not (logically) to have discovered a compulsion; it is only to have discovered an explanation or part of an explanation. As psychology advances, therefore, and discovers more and more causes, we should not naturally expect that all these causes should fall into the category of 'outside' causes or compulsions. We should rather expect that, as psychologists made clear to us the causes or explanations of various actions, we could place them under their appropriate headings of 'inside' or 'outside', and the actions to which they gave rise under the headings of 'free' or 'compelled'. If we feel bound to categorise any cause which has been explained to us as compulsive, something has gone wrong with our criteria; for there is nothing in the notion of cause itself which involves compulsion.

Here, then, we have what may be described as a situation involving philosophic doubt. But before trying to resolve it, let us be clear just how much of our problem can be removed by philosophy, and how much by factual discovery. We must accept the fact that we cannot always, or even usually, know which of our actions are free and which are compelled. We cannot know this in the case of any action of whose causes we are ignorant; for since we do not know its cause, we do not know whether its cause is 'inside' or 'outside'. It may be a compulsive cause; and though once we know the cause we need to use our criteria for putting it in its proper category, we also have to be aware of the psychological nature of the cause in order to use those criteria correctly. Unless we can explain an action, we cannot know whether it is free or not. Thus, if the man in our example took off his coat because he was hot and wanted to take it off, we might perhaps wish to call his action 'free'; whereas if he took off his coat because of a hypnotic suggestion, we should certainly call it 'compulsive'. This is a question of empirical fact, which we should have to be able to answer before we could categorise his action.

Let us imagine a situation in which we should certainly want to say that a man's action was free, even though we knew its causes. Suppose a man had the chance of breaking a promise, but did in fact keep it, because of his sense of honour and obligation; and suppose that nothing which would in everyone's eyes count as compulsion was being applied to him. It must be granted that to say that he kept his promise 'because of his sense of honour' is not to give a full explanation. In order to do this, we should have to trace back the causes of his having a sense of honour; and since no man is born with a sense of honour, we should come to the conclusion that his sense of honour was due to some 'outside' cause. We could sensibly say that, as a child, he was compelled to acquire a sense of honour, in the sense that, conditions of heredity and environment being what they were, he could not have done otherwise. Considerations of this kind tempt us to say that none of our actions can be free. For since all men, ultimately, are entirely the products of heredity and environment, it must be admitted that if we trace the causes for their actions sufficiently far back, we shall always arrive at 'outside' causes. Thus we could argue, of the man in our example, that to defend his action as free on the grounds that a sense of honour is an 'inside' cause is merely short-sighted; for that sense of honour is itself the product of 'outside' causes. Yet despite all this, it still seems that we should want to say that the action was free.

It is clear, therefore, that the criterion of 'inside' and 'outside' causes requires explanation and enlargement before it can be accepted as satisfactory. We must at least try to answer the question 'What counts as an "inside" cause, and what as an "outside" cause?' To this, various answers have been given by philosophers; but for the most part they have been biased by their notions of 'true freedom' or the 'truly free' man. Undoubtedly freedom is something which we cherish, and compulsion something which we wish to avoid: but this is no reason for classifying all causes which operate for good as 'inside' causes productive of freedom, and all causes which operate for evil as 'outside' and compulsive causes. Plato, for example, believed that man was only 'really' free when governed by his reason; but it is more accurate to say that Plato wished to monopolise the word 'free' for the sole benefit of men who were so governed. Aristotle more sensibly says that we consider that the irrational feelings are just as much a part of human nature as the reason, so that the actions arising from them belong to the man who does them (i.e. are the product of 'inside' causes).

The persuasive efforts of such philosophers as Plato are significant, however, inasmuch as they point the way to the crux of the problem. These efforts amount to adopting a special picture of the human 'self'. Thus for Plato the true self is the rational self; anything which interferes with this counts with him as compulsion. The important point to be noticed here is that the application of the criterion of 'inside' and 'outside' causes, and hence of the use of 'free' and 'compelled', depends upon a tacit reference to a 'self' or a 'person' who is or is not being compelled. Consequently, if you wish to impose your application of the criterion on others, you must also impose upon them your picture of the 'self'. This is precisely what happens in everyday arguments about freedom. Thus, suppose I wish to maintain that a man who steals something did not act freely. I might first try to claim that he was driven, by the use of physical force (e.g. at the point of a bayonet), to steal. If this is not true, however, I might claim that he suffered from kleptomania. If this is not true, I might claim that the temptations he felt were overwhelmingly strong. If this is not true, I might claim that though he had a very bad character, he could not help having it, because of his heredity or education. As we saw in the case of the man who kept his promise from a sense of honour, these claims are bound to succeed at some point, since men are ultimately the products of their heredity and environment. But as I make one claim after another, I have to narrow my picture of the man's 'self' in a way which, after a certain point, may come to seem absurd.

Linguistically, this is a question of how we use personal pronouns and nouns. If I say 'He was compelled to fall, because he was pushed', I use 'he' to include both the mind and the body of the man I am talking about. If I say 'He was compelled to fall, because he has an obsession about jumping off high places', I use 'he' to refer to part of, or certain aspects of, the man's mind, but not all: for I exclude his obsession. If I say 'He was compelled to fall, because of his strong desire to jump', I similarly exclude his desire from his 'self'. And at this point my picture of the 'self', which here excludes desires, seems at least unusual. What I am doing is deliberately setting out to diminish the area of the man's 'self'—to restrict my use of 'he' more and more closely—so that I can then confidently assert that the cause of the man's falling was outside 'him'.

Perhaps this point can be clarified by a brief consideration of our uses of 'free' when we are not referring to people; as for instance when we refer to a wheel running 'freely'. We mean by this that the wheel is not prevented or hindered from acting in the way in which we expect it to act; and we have no difficulty in determining whether this is so or not. For we always know what to count as 'outside' interference, or as 'inside' causes for the wheel's behaving in a particular way. This is because we always use the word 'wheel', and pronouns which stand in place of 'wheel', to describe the same things. 'Wheel' includes, and always includes, the hub, felloe, and spokes. Consequently, if for example a wheel is not running smoothly, we know when to say 'It's the wheel's fault: the spokes are bent', and when to say 'It's not the wheel's fault: the axle isn't oiled properly'. We feel no temptation to diminish the area of reference of 'wheel': it would be absurd to say 'the wheel was compelled to wobble because the spokes were bent'. For this would imply a picture of some kind of 'inner wheel', distinct from (and hence able to be compelled by) parts of the wheel such as the spokes.

In this example, we could truly say that the wheel itself was responsible for its wobbling; it was running 'freely', but it was an inefficient wheel. The fact that we could trace back the causes for the spokes being bent, and hence for the wobbling, to factors outside the wheel does not worry us. Somebody may have bent the spokes by hitting them; and this is certainly not the wheel's fault. But this does not mean that the wobbling is not the wheel's fault; for whether the spokes are bent or not, and for whatever cause they are bent, they still count as part of the wheel. The wheel, therefore, is responsible for whatever happens as a result of the bent spokes. The bent spokes are an 'inside' cause.

But when we speak of 'a man' being compelled or acting freely, or say 'he was compelled' or 'he acted freely', it is never quite clear what we are describing by 'man' or 'he'. It has not generally been observed how far the picture of an 'inner self' has affected our language. In particular we are apt to be misled by possessive adjectives such as 'his'. We can list, albeit in a rough and ready fashion, the various factors or 'parts' of the human mind— 'desire', 'reason', 'determination', 'sense of duty', and so on. Then we refer to 'his desire', 'his reason', 'his determination', etc.: and this use of 'his' suggests an 'inner self' which possesses, controls, or can be controlled by, these various factors or 'parts'. By this usage, it is always possible for us to regard any cause as 'outside', by the simple expedient of using 'he' or 'his' in a way that seems logically to exclude the cause mentioned. Sometimes this usage seems obviously absurd, as it would if I were to say 'He did not do it freely: his will compelled him to do it', or 'His reason compelled him to do it'. But owing to the deceptive influence of the 'inner self' picture, any slightly less obvious absurdity there may be is not generally noticed.

Even if we do not allow ourselves to be deceived by the 'inner self' myth, however, we may still find the same difficulties. A deliberate shrinking of the area of the 'self',

5-2

in order to classify a cause as 'outside', is only one of the ways in which we may deny responsibility. Instead of diminishing the area, we may change its shape. If we say 'He was compelled by his desires', we need not necessarily be withdrawing into a mythical 'inner self', and using 'he' in such a way as to exclude all possible causes. We may use it to include a great many things—reason, determination, etc.—but to exclude desire. Again, if we want to say 'He was compelled by his determination', we might include reason and desire within the circle of 'he', but exclude determination. In this way, we perch ourselves, as it were, on some part of ourselves which is not the cause of our actions, and disown the part which is the cause; and then when we come across other cases of possible responsibility which might seem to threaten our perch, we jump off it and on to another: thus allowing ourselves to disown our previous one. This sort of picture of the 'self', or of a 'person', shifts and changes to suit our own convenience.

We can now begin to see in what way our anxiety is unnecessary. Provided we keep our criteria of the 'self', and our use of pronouns such as 'he', constant and unchanging, and provided we have the knowledge to identify the cause of any action, we shall have no difficulty in classifying the cause as 'inside' or 'outside'. 'Inside' causes are those which arise from within the 'self'—which are part of 'him'—and 'outside' causes are those which arise from outside the 'self', and are not part of 'him'. Aristotle's criteria for freedom are perfectly satisfactory, provided we adhere to constant criteria for the 'self'. The reason why we tend to be worried by the advance of psychology is that the clinical and scientific approach of psychology to human behaviour cannot afford to adopt constant criteria for the 'self'. Psychology is not concerned simply with determining whether the cause of any action lies inside or outside an individual; it is concerned with isolating and analysing whatever the cause may be. This process of isolation and extrapolation has had a profound effect on our everyday language. We tend to think of the human personality as a bundle of known or unknown psychological factors, for none of which the 'man' himself is responsible. When we have explained a man's action—say, as the result of kleptomania—we tend *ipso facto* to dissociate the man from the factors involved in our explanation. Kleptomania, we unconsciously assume, is no part of the man: it must be an 'outside' cause or compulsion.

The fact is that, once we know the causes of a man's action, a question like 'Did he act freely?' or 'Was he responsible for his action?' is partly a verbal one, the answer to which depends on our criteria for the word 'he'. If we include kleptomania as part of what we mean by 'he', then the answer is that he did act freely, for it is nonsense to say that a man can be compelled by himself; and as we have already seen, the fact that he may have been compelled to acquire kleptomania is irrelevant. For whatever may have been responsible for the kleptomania, the kleptomania is responsible for the action; and on these criteria, the kleptomania counts as part of the man.

This is not to suggest that the whole matter is entirely arbitrary. There are important social and personal considerations which would persuade us to adopt some criteria for the personality and reject others. Thus to include kleptomania as part of what we mean by 'he' when we say '"he" did it' would be misleading: for to say 'he did it' or 'it was his fault' might suggest that we can properly blame or punish him, and this we do not wish to do. It would not be factually incorrect, nor logically absurd: but it would be pragmatically unwise.[1]

Nor is it necessary, as some philosophers have supposed, to be able to say truly of a man's action 'He could have acted (or chosen) otherwise' if we are to classify his action as free. This notion also depends on a misleading picture of an 'inner self'. Once we know the full explanation of a man's action, we can only mean by 'He could have acted otherwise', 'He could have or would have acted otherwise, if conditions had been different'; and this statement seems rather trivial. As Nowell-Smith writes, '..."could have" statements can be refuted...by showing that some necessary condition was absent...';[2] and this is precisely what an advance in psychological knowledge might be able to do in the case of any action. But the fact that a man could not have acted otherwise—and this is simply to say that we know the full explanation for his action—does not diminish his freedom or his responsibility. For it is the man himself who acted; he was not compelled to act by something outside himself.

It will perhaps be objected that this is to reduce human freedom to the same level as the 'freedom' of inanimate objects. But this objection is unfair. It is both true and important that when we talk of men acting freely and wheels running freely, we are using 'freely' in the same *sense*, that is, to mean 'without external compulsion or constraint'. The same applies to 'responsible'. But this does not mean that the causes from which men act when they are free are the same as the causes from which wheels act when they are free. Thus it makes sense to talk of a man's 'motive' for a free action, whereas wheels do not have motives. Men are in control of their actions, or

---

[1] See pp. 74–83.   [2] Nowell-Smith, *Ethics*, p. 276.

responsible for their actions, in the same *sense* that a wheel is responsible for the way in which it runs; but the two are not responsible in the same *way*. We might wish to express this, perhaps, by saying that men have a wider range of causes from which they can act freely; that whereas wheels act in ways which need only a limited knowledge of physical science to explain them, the explanation of human actions covers far more ground. Moreover, the concept of human freedom is logically prior to the concept of the freedom of inanimate objects, and can indeed only be extended to inanimate objects by a kind of metaphor. We grant freedom to wheels only by analogy, though this does not mean that we are misusing language when we speak of wheels running freely. It does not mean that we are reducing human freedom to an inanimate level: rather have we granted inanimate objects the privilege of being spoken of in terms derived from human behaviour.

(b) *Criteria of Morality*

In attempting to define moral virtue, Aristotle says that it is a 'disposition to choose', and in another passage connects it with 'voluntary actions, for which praise and blame are given'. This analysis has won general acceptance among philosophers; and some, indeed, have gone so far as to say that it is the actual effectiveness of praise and blame, or reward and punishment, which constitutes the criterion of moral actions and traits of character. This same criterion would also be used to distinguish between what we call a 'virtue' on the one hand, and a 'talent', or 'a piece of good fortune' on the other; or between a 'vice' and a 'misfortune'. I wish to argue that this criterion is unsatisfactory, and that the distinction with which we are all familiar between moral and non-moral actions and traits is not in fact founded upon any secure *logical* basis at all.

Let us first consider the view that an action's being voluntary, or the agent's acting freely, is a necessary or sufficient condition for the action being classed as 'moral'. To say that a man acted freely, as has been pointed out in the last section, is to say that the cause of his action was an 'inside' cause: that 'he', and not something outside 'him', was responsible for the action. Thus, the view claims that a man's action comes into the category of morality if the cause for the action was 'inside' him; and presumably, a moral trait is a disposition to do such actions from such causes. If such causes operate, we can praise and blame: if not, we can only envy or sympathise.

We should notice at once that this cannot be a sufficient condition to determine a moral issue: for there are many actions which arise from inside causes—many free actions—which we should certainly not want to describe as moral. For example, it is now a matter of choice with me whether I read over the last sentence which I have written or whether I do not, whether I touch my left knee or my right, or neither, and so on. To describe these as moral actions would be to abolish the existing distinction altogether.

Nor can it be held that the operation of 'inside' causes is even a necessary condition for an action's being moral, or for moral traits. For it often happens—I would say it usually happens—that we do not know the cause (or all the causes) for a man's acting in a certain way. Since we do not know what the cause is, we cannot classify it as 'inside' or 'outside'; and hence we cannot know whether the man acted freely or not. We have, indeed, a prejudice in favour of regarding all actions as free, or as proceeding from 'inside' causes, until we have identified them as compulsive; but this is only a prejudice. To say that a man acted freely is not to say that we do not know of any 'outside' cause operating upon him: it is to say that there was in fact no 'outside' cause. And whatever picture we may have of 'a man', or a man's 'self', we cannot know whether the cause falls 'inside' that picture, until we know what the cause is. Yet in a great many of such cases (and such cases are very common) we still feel ourselves entitled to say that the action was a moral one, or that the disposition (we do not know whether freely or compulsively acquired) was a moral disposition. We may often be at a loss to account for or explain why a man steals, murders, or perjures himself; but we have no difficulty in placing these actions within the sphere of morality.

It may be asked why in that case we do not consider kleptomaniacs as immoral: this seems to suggest that acting freely is a necessary criterion for morality. We must not be misled here by an ambiguity in the word 'moral'. Our concern in the present context is to determine which matters are moral matters (as opposed to matters of taste or matters of fact, for instance): but there is a common use of the word whereby it means 'good or right in a moral way'—the opposite of 'immoral'. We use the first sense in trying to describe or categorise an action or a disposition, and the second when we wish to praise or condemn. Thus we would be perfectly prepared to answer the question 'Is a disposition to steal a moral trait?' in the affirmative, without reference to why the disposition exists—whether or not it is compulsive; but we do not blame a man, like the kleptomaniac, whose disposition is compulsive, or call him 'immoral', because he did not act freely. In other words, the actual *application* of the words 'moral' and 'immoral', used as terms of praise or blame, may indeed depend logically upon freedom and responsibility: but to *categorise* an action or disposition as 'moral' or 'non-moral' need not involve us with freedom or responsibility at all.

The connection between praise and blame on the one hand, and freedom and responsibility on the other, is also not quite so clear-cut as some philosophers have thought. It is true that one can (logically) only blame a person if he is responsible for his actions: otherwise one would not be blaming the person, but something 'outside' the person. But this only means that whether we blame a person, and whether we say that he was acting freely, depend logically on how we use the words 'person' and 'he'. As I have said previously (p. 69) this does not mean that our criteria for blame or freedom are purely arbitrary. To say that a person acted freely implies the possibility of blame, which in turn implies that blame might be desirable: it might deter him from future actions of the same kind, set a good example to others, and so forth. In cases where we are sure that blame is useless, we tend to adjust our criteria to exclude the possibility of blame, and hence of freedom. This adjustment of criteria is obviously important from a practical point of view, when we are thinking about rewards and punishments. But there is nothing nonsensical or logically absurd in choosing whatever criteria we wish. Indeed, it is plain that these criteria are likely to vary according to our purposes: it may be best for the law-courts to use one set of criteria for freedom and responsibility, the psychoanalyst another set, and so on. We may ask ourselves 'Is it wiser to consider this man's action in terms of freedom and responsibility, or in terms of health and disease?': but there is no general answer to this question. Our answer in particular cases will depend on our relationship to the man and our general purposes.

Thus the logical connection (between the application of the words 'moral' or 'immoral' and freedom) serves an obvious sociological purpose. We do not want to describe a homicidal maniac as immoral, because we want to treat him as a sufferer and not as an agent. It is not nonsense to use the words 'moral' and 'immoral' in such cases—indeed, many people do use them—but it is beside the point. In the same way, if someone tells a thoroughly justifiable lie, a 'white lie', we do not call this immoral, because here too (though for a different reason) we do not consider it profitable to think in the category of morality. Note that we do not call homicidal maniacs or white lies 'moral', any more than we call them 'immoral': we simply avoid the terminology altogether, because we are interested in other things beside morality.

It is presumably this sort of reasoning which has led philosophers to regard the actual effectiveness of praise, blame, reward and punishment as a criterion of morality. It can be shown fairly easily that this effectiveness cannot act as a sufficient condition for an action's being moral. In the first place, we are often in doubt whether praise, etc. are effective or not, since we do not know the causes of the original action, and have insufficient evidence to assess whether or not our treatment is effective. Indeed, we commonly praise and blame people (such as case-hardened criminals) when we know quite well that our verdict will have no effect whatsoever. And secondly, traits which we should not consider moral traits can be affected by these verdicts and types of treatment. People can be encouraged to acquire good taste by judicious

75

praise and blame; and even the behaviour of dogs can be affected by rewards and punishments.

It can alternatively be claimed that the effectiveness of praise, etc. is a necessary condition for an action's being moral. That is, whenever an action is moral, praise or blame is effective. Thus Nowell-Smith writes 'We might therefore say that moral traits of character are just those traits that are known to be amenable to praise or blame'.[1] But here too we are liable to a confusion between the two senses of 'moral' mentioned earlier. We can perfectly well categorise an action as moral or non-moral without having the least idea whether praise or blame will be effective in any particular case, or indeed without having any particular case in mind at all; and we can also praise an action as moral or condemn it as immoral without knowing (or even considering) whether the person who did the action will respond properly to our praise or condemnation. In neither sense, therefore, is it true that the effectiveness of praise or blame is a *sine qua non*.

Those who hold this view have been misled by the general tendency to restrict morality to issues which are amenable to praise and blame, reward and punishment. But this restriction is not carried out consistently, and still less has it dominated our language to the extent of making 'amenable to praise, etc.' part of the meaning of 'moral'. The truth is that we do not know, in most cases, whether praise, etc. is efficacious, because of our psychological ignorance; but this does not prevent us from classifying some actions as non-moral and others as moral. It is only with the greatest reluctance that we exclude an action or a trait from the concept of morality, as with kleptomania. The practical reason for our doing this, as

[1] Nowell-Smith, *Ethics*, pp. 302–10.

we have already seen, is that we do not see any point in keeping it within the concept if there is no point in punishing or blaming it. And even this shows a considerable degree of enlightenment: we have developed since the days when primitive peoples blamed and punished inanimate objects. Men have always praised and blamed; but they have not always concerned themselves with what types of treatment are effective.

It is worth noticing that we can do more than categorise actions and dispositions under the general headings of 'moral' and 'non-moral'. We can also specify which actions and dispositions are 'moral' and which 'immoral': and this without making use of praise and blame. In doing this we should be using 'moral' and 'immoral' as purely descriptive terms, not applying them as terms of praise and blame to any particular case. We should be simply describing certain behaviour-patterns to which, in a particular community, praise and blame were usually attached. Thus we can say that keeping promises and telling the truth are 'moral' things to do in this society: and that stealing, lying, murdering and so forth are 'immoral'. Naturally these words have overtones of value, since part of their function is to praise or blame when they are actually applied to particular cases: but it is legitimate to use them purely as terms of description or categorisation. Thus we may say to a young child 'That's stealing' when he takes an apple from a shop, even though we might not want to blame him for doing it: we are here informing him that his action is one of a class of immoral actions. In other words, it is plainly possible to *list* a number of actions which we should want to call 'moral' or 'immoral' purely as a matter of sociology. This too suggests that what counts as a moral issue is a matter of sociological fact rather than a matter of logic, and can only be settled by reference to certain empirical facts: briefly, we might say, by seeing whether it is regarded by the community of which the individual concerned is a member in a 'moral light'. What we have to do, therefore, is to determine what it is for an issue to be regarded in a 'moral light'.

What is regarded as a moral issue notoriously varies from age to age, and from community to community. Eating beans, displaying various parts of the body, not going to church, and a wide variety of other practices have been regarded as moral issues, but are not now so regarded. We must realise that there is no single 'right answer' to the question of what is a moral issue and what is not. It would be absurd to deny that working on the Sabbath was a question of morality to the ancient Hebrews, and equally absurd to deny that it is generally not a question of morality elsewhere. We can certainly ask the question 'Were they right to regard it as a moral issue?'; but any reasons which we should give for a negative answer to this question would be adduced merely to support our own distinction between various issues. And these reasons would not be derived from language, but from our own moral values as they apply to the world of practical affairs. Thus, we might say 'It does not matter whether you work on the Sabbath or not', or 'It's not worth making a fuss about it', or 'Working on the Sabbath is just a matter of individual taste'.

A moral issue is not a matter of taste, from which it differs in at least two respects. First, the fact that we call something a moral issue implies the existence of moral standards (usually those standards which are currently accepted within a particular community) or of some kind of moral authority. And secondly, moral issues are *important* in a way that does not apply to matters of taste, or more precisely are thought to be important by those who consider them to be moral issues. But it does not follow from this that moral issues are those issues about which we make judgements which we are prepared, as philosophers sometimes put it, to 'universalise'. We may well be prepared to universalise our ultimate standards, or highest ends, or top-level criteria: thus we may say that all men ought to pursue happiness, or act from a sense of duty. But morality is concerned with our actions and behaviour on a far lower level; and here circumstances alter cases, so that the notion of applying our judgement universally becomes useless. For example, we believe that a man ought not to steal important documents belonging to his country, though he ought (under certain circumstances) to steal them from his country's enemies. We cannot make a universal judgement about stealing. But this does not alter the fact that stealing is a moral matter.

Certain issues are regarded in a 'moral light', I suggest, simply because they are the issues which a community regards as important, and as backed by some kind of authority. There are obvious methods of discovering what a community regards in a 'moral light'. The simplest is merely to observe which issues are spoken of as 'moral' within that community. Another is to see whether people in general are apt to react strongly to certain behaviour, to express indignant disapproval of it, or to punish it. A third is to consider what types of behaviour are approved of and encouraged, or disapproved of and discouraged, by the laws and conventions of the community: for, in general, the connection between these and morality is very close. An immoral action, like a criminal or a highly unconventional action, tends to shock people. Children learn the difference between morality and matters of taste, not by observing what behaviour is voluntary or can be effectively punished, and much less by any intuitive appreciation of the distinction: but by observing what shocks their elders and what does not.

For historical reasons, among which we may legitimately list the rise of Protestant Christianity and the influence of Kantian ethics, we have evidently decided to draw a very sharp dividing line between moral and non-moral issues. To us, a moral issue (as the derivation of the word implies) is connected, albeit loosely connected, with such concepts as a man's character, will, sense of duty, conscience, and so forth. So we usually, though not always, restrict moral issues to issues where men act freely, and can be praised, blamed, rewarded or punished; since we always like to include character, will, conscience, etc., as part of the human 'self'. These, we believe, are things that a man is never without, and which all men share: unlike talents or diseases, which are beyond our individual control.

Some of us still have, and most of us speak as if we had, a picture of the 'self' which includes all those factors which we believe to be operative in moral issues. But it is our distinction between moral and non-moral issues which is logically prior: we tailor our picture of the 'self' to fit the distinction, and our tailoring is often rather shoddy. We say, in effect, 'These issues are moral issues, and the rest are not. It would be intolerable to suppose, except in very unusual cases, that men are not responsible for their moral choices; so we shall therefore cling determinedly to a certain picture of what a "man" is, a picture which allows us to preserve the belief that men are responsible.' We could hold this view without anxiety until the development of psychology showed us that there is often a conflict between those issues which we want to call moral, and those issues

where we should want to say that a man was praiseworthy
or blameworthy: that there is sometimes no point in
praising or blaming a man who acted immorally.

All this arises because we consider moral issues to have
a special importance, as we have already seen. The causes
for our thinking this provide a study for psychologists
or historians; but a possible justification for this view
might be that these issues are of particular relevance in the
attempt to achieve higher ends or standards which we
think important. In fact, however, such a justification
might carry little weight in practice, since men do not
usually adopt the distinction between moral and non-
moral issues from rational motives, but by imitation and
custom. Thus many people believe that happiness is more
important than sexual orthodoxy; but sexual perversion
shocks us more than unhappiness, and sexual behaviour
is a moral issue whereas happiness, generally, is not. Again,
it is a moral issue whether we steal or not: but it is not
a moral issue whether or not we give great thought to
abolishing theft by political measures. Yet the latter might
well be thought to be of more ultimate importance, in
reference to whatever ends honesty is supposed to satisfy,
than the former. Moral issues, at least in all countries
which are Christian or nominally such, are generally
speaking issues of individual, person-to-person behaviour,
and do not extend to politics. This is simply because we
believe (or used to believe) that it is the individual's
personal behaviour that counts for most: what he does
with his 'soul', 'will', or 'character', and how much
attention he pays to his 'conscience'.

To distinguish moral from non-moral issues by a sociological criterion is not to devalue morality, but rather to
demonstrate its proper function. As we shall see later in

this chapter, one of the functions of Moralism is to preserve the established order of society: and it is for this reason that morality is usually restricted to a sphere of action which an average individual in society would normally be expected to understand and master. Thus it would be expected of an average person that he should carry out what we may call his 'local' obligations, that is, that he should be loyal to his parents and his country, not steal from his fellows, and assist those who were ill or starving if their cases came to his immediate notice. But it would not be expected of him that he should be loyal to humanity, or that he should greatly concern himself with people who were ill or starving in far-off countries: indeed, we should hardly call these 'obligations' at all. There *need* be no logic behind this: it may, in fact, often be more important for a man to forget his local obligations, and devote his attention to wider issues (such as preventing world war, assisting the people of other countries, and so on). But such things would not be included within the sphere of duty or obligation or morality, except in a wider (and consequently a weaker) sense of these words. For morality, and the specifically moral terminology which includes 'duty' and 'obligation', is not intended to cover such cases: it is intended only as a good working policy for ordinary people, with the abilities and characters that ordinary people have. It is none the worse for that: but it would be a grave mistake to suppose, as many philosophers and perhaps almost all ordinary people have supposed, that this sociologically important function is logically valuable in other contexts. The morality of a society may be sociologically essential for its preservation, but may still be quite useless as a guide for what a man really ought to do. We shall go into this more closely in the next section.

To sum up, we must distinguish between the following activities:

(*a*) Assessing the worth of an action or a trait of character: what we may call appraising it.

(*b*) Assessing whether the action or trait is moral or non-moral: what we may call classifying it, by accepted empirical evidence (observing the customs of a given society).

(*c*) Assessing whether the agent is responsible, and consequently being able to praise or blame him, and to stigmatise him as 'moral' or 'immoral'.

(*d*) Assessing whether a particular type of treatment— indignation, encouragement, punishment or reward— will have the desired effect on the agent.

Of these, (*a*) is simply a question of our values (both moral and non-moral); (*b*) is a question of empirical fact; (*c*) involves both finding the cause of an action, and deciding whether or not to include it within our picture of a 'person': and unless we do this, we cannot (logically) praise or blame him; (*d*) is again a question of empirical fact, indeed of scientific expertise. It is a question for the psychologist or the sociologist—provided we agree about what 'the desired effect' is, which of course is a question of value, and throws us back to (*a*).

(*c*) *The Function of Moral Principles*

Philosophers have paid a great deal of attention to words which have a very wide application in moral discourse, such as 'good', 'ought', 'right', 'duty', etc., and rather less attention to words which represent moral principles which have a limited application, such as 'loyalty', 'truthfulness', 'justice', 'honesty', and so on. Yet in moral arguments (or what look like arguments) it is words of the second type which play by far the largest part. Practical moral discourse, in fact, together with moral exhortation, praise, condemnation and advice, seems to find phrases like 'You ought not to do that', 'This is good' or 'It is right to do the other', too weak and colourless to be effective. We prefer to pass judgement in more direct terms, as when we say 'That's stealing', 'It was most disloyal of him to have said that', 'He told a lie', or 'That decision was unjust'. Even in their earliest years children are introduced to, and display a remarkably firm grasp of, certain limited moral concepts; they understand very well what is meant by 'stealing', 'lying' and 'fair play', for example. Yet it is not at all clear precisely what purpose is served by the principles based on such concepts, or how the words which express them play a significant part in moral discourse.

Even the actual usage of words like 'stealing' and 'lying' is not as clear as we sometimes seem to think. It is commonly believed that such words possess both a descriptive and an evaluative element of meaning; and indeed it seems impossible to deny this. For we can only apply the word 'stealing' to actions which have certain empirical or factual characteristics (taking something which is the legal property of somebody else), which shows that it has descriptive meaning; and equally it seems that when we use the word we intend it as a criticism or a reproach, which shows that it is used to evaluate. We might say, then, that we could translate any of these limited moral words by giving its descriptive meaning plus a moral condemnation or commendation; and this seems to work quite well for at least some such words. The distinction between 'killing' and 'murder', for instance, seems to be simply that 'murder' means 'killing when it is wrong to kill' or 'killing which is morally wicked'. Hence we do not speak of soldiers fighting for their country or of judges who pass the death sentence as 'murdering'.

But this analysis is not really satisfactory. Two points in particular seem to suggest that it requires revision. First, what are we to make of statements which express the moral principles which we are discussing, such as 'Stealing is wrong' or 'It is wicked to tell lies'? If 'stealing' means 'taking property which is legally another's when it is wrong to do so' (a simple mixture of descriptive plus evaluative meaning), and if 'lying' means 'saying what is not true when it is morally wicked to do so', these two statements become simple tautologies. This looks very odd. A statement which means 'Taking property which is legally another's when it is wrong to do so is wrong' does not seem very helpful, and 'Stealing is wrong' is certainly not intended as a tautology of this kind. Secondly, it seems as if we can use at least some of these words as equivalent to a set of characteristics which are purely factual. Surely the empirical statement 'He took property which legally belonged to another', with whatever additions we may think necessary ('without the intention to return it', 'without the man's consent', etc.), does justify us in saying 'He stole'. Similarly 'He deliberately said what was untrue', with other empirical additions such as 'when his hearer was likely to think that it was true', does entail 'He lied'. To take a final example, it seems that one is compelled to say of the father in the parable of the Prodigal Son that he acted unjustly in welcoming his undeserving son so lavishly, in contrast to the way he treated the elder brother: for an unjust action is precisely an action which does not give people what they deserve.

Now as the last example shows, this lands us in serious difficulties; for there are plenty of cases where we should want to approve of actions having those factual characteristics which seem to entail calling them 'stealing', 'lying', 'injustice' and so on. A starving beggar who takes a loaf of bread from a shop without paying for it is unquestionably stealing; a spy may lie to the enemy in war-time; a humanitarian judge may make decisions that are unjust. Yet we might approve of all these actions. We seem, therefore, to be committed to saying 'This is unjust (dishonest, untruthful, etc.) but I approve of it'. And this might well appear to be contradictory. In other words, how are we to account for the fact that these limited words, such as 'dishonest', 'unjust' and so on, carry an element of disapproval, although we sometimes want to approve of actions to which they are applicable?

It is worth noticing that by far the most common attempt to escape from this position, made by philosophers as well as ordinary people, involves trying to alter the meanings of these limited words so that they become inapplicable to the cases under discussion. This is probably because, for psychological reasons which we need not discuss, most people dislike having to make exceptions to their moral principles, and are to some extent hypnotised by words like 'just', 'honest', 'loyal' and so on; they resent any attempt either to reject their moral implications or to set them aside altogether. Thus Plato dissociates justice from the notion of requital, which certainly violates common Greek usage; and on a less exalted level, we might well say of a starving beggar who takes a loaf of bread 'I don't call that stealing'. One can see this process in operation in the phrase 'a white lie'. When a man tells his hostess untruly that he has enjoyed a party, we are bound to admit by the established empirical criteria that this is a lie; but by incorporating 'lie' into the stock phrase 'a white lie' we rob it of its accustomed moral implications.

However, this loophole does not lead anywhere, since it involves a distortion of ordinary language which can be easily criticised. We are bound to accept the empirical criteria for lying, stealing, justice and so on. We must, therefore, challenge the supposed moral implications of these words. And once we realise that the element of value in them exists only by implication, and not as part of their meaning, part of the difficulty disappears. We cannot say 'That is good, but I do not approve of it': this is nonsense, because 'good' does not only *suggest* 'I approve': it necessarily *entails* it. But we can say 'That is just, but I do not approve of it', because 'just' only *suggests* 'I approve'. When approving of actions which are dishonest, unjust, etc. we deliberately reject the suggestion or implication; and it is always open to us to do this without contradiction. This distinction also explains the value and use of apparent tautologies such as 'Stealing is wrong'. This is not a tautology, but has the function of making an implicit judgement explicit: 'stealing' implies condemnation, and the addition of 'is wrong' asserts it.

The importation into moral arguments of moral principles which are dependent on these limited words acts as a kind of initial attack upon the value of the proposed action. If I say of the beggar taking a loaf of bread 'But that's stealing' this is an attack in the sense that I am, in effect, saying 'This action would be stealing: it is usually wrong to steal (or, other things being equal it is wrong to steal): so if we are going to approve of this action we shall have to prove it to be an exception to this general rule (or, we shall have to prove that other things are not equal)'. In this respect, saying 'But that's stealing' is rather like saying of a chess player who deliberately sacrifices his queen, for instance, 'But that's very unorthodox'. The implication is that he is acting wrongly or foolishly unless—which is still an open question—he has some good reason for so acting, for example, that he is going as a result to mate in three moves. Calling something 'stealing', like calling it 'unorthodox', implies condemnation which is not withdrawn unless there is good reason to withdraw it.

But although this is plainly a fair description of the logical function of such principles, it is still not at all clear what value can be assigned to this function in moral discussion. It is more difficult to determine the usefulness of principles than their usage. In certain cases, admittedly, they have an obvious value. I may say, for instance, to a child who takes an apple from a greengrocer's stall without paying for it 'You mustn't do that, dear, that's stealing'. Here I assume that the child is conditioned against doing actions which can correctly be called 'stealing'; and what I am doing is simply to inform the child that this counts as an action of this kind. The child has not yet properly learnt the empirical characteristics which go to make up stealing. But in the case of adults we may presume a proper knowledge of these empirical characteristics; and it is not easy to see what can be gained by simply asserting that a particular action possesses them. Surely this knowledge would be common to both parties in a discussion.

Let us suppose that I am considering whether a starving beggar ought to take a loaf of bread without paying for it, and let us see what purpose could be served by my being told that this is stealing. In such a case, I may react in various ways, which suggest that I was in one state of mind or another when I originally considered the question.

(1) Like the child, I may be unaware or temporarily forgetful that this action counts as stealing, whilst accepting the general principle that stealing is wrong.

(2) I may not accept the principle that stealing is wrong.

(3) I may be wondering whether this is an exception to the principle.

All these are possible cases, though the first is very unlikely, and the third improbable. It is sufficiently plain that it is only in (1) that my being told that the action is stealing will be of any help. Telling me this acts primarily as a reminder that it is generally believed that actions with certain empirical characteristics lie open to condemnation. This reminder is only useful in (1). For in (2) I can retort that though the principle that stealing is wrong is generally believed, I do not myself believe it; and in (3) I can reply that it is precisely this point which I am considering, namely whether the action is really to be condemned or not: whether or not it is an exception to the general principle.

Drawing attention to a moral principle provides us with a reason for a moral judgement in this sense, therefore: that it reminds us that we have at least some evidence on the question. If we accept that X is a case of stealing, and that most cases of stealing are wrong, then in default of further evidence it is the most reasonable course to disapprove of X and avoid doing it. This is a matter of simple probability: it is more likely that X is not an exception than that it is one. Most of our habitual moral behaviour depends on the validity of this argument; and occasionally, as in case (1), we need to be reminded of it.

But in cases of moral doubt its use is limited or even non-existent; for most cases of this kind, like case (3), consist precisely in wondering whether X is an exception or not. If we were not wondering—if we were not in doubt—we should automatically subsume X under the general rule, as in fact we do unconsciously hundreds of times every day.

In this kind of moral discussion, there is no point in discussing whether the considered action is stealing or not: probably agreement about this has already been reached. What we do is simply to consider the facts, and see if they suggest that the action would be justified in the light of some other moral principle. Some of these facts, no doubt, will be those on which the rule against stealing relies for its general validity. Thus, in discussing the case of the beggar, we may point out that his action might tend to disrupt society by removing public confidence in the safety of personal possessions, that he might get a severe prison sentence, and so on. But we have temporarily shelved the condemnatory implications in the word 'stealing'; and it is significant that we do not take them off the shelf again if we decide to approve of the action. We tend, on the contrary, to forget about them completely, and to avoid the word which contains them. Thus, to return to our previous example, we could say of the action of the Prodigal Son's father: 'That was unjust, but right.' This is not contradictory; but in fact we never want to say it, for the simple reason that 'unjust' implies condemnation whenever it is used, and in this case we do not want to condemn at all. It is not at all a question of our wishing to deny that the action was unjust (though there is a perennial temptation to do this): on the contrary, we could be forced to admit it. It is simply a question of our not wishing to say so.

Nearly all cases of serious moral discussion or doubt, I believe, are like case (3), where we are wondering whether the action is exceptional or not. We are, in effect, trying to treat the case on its own merits: to consider all facts relevant to it before coming to a moral decision. When we are doing this, the introduction of moral principles depending upon notions such as stealing, honesty, loyalty, justice and so on hampers rather than assists the discussion, because they have the effect of prejudging the issue. If an action can fairly be described as stealing, dishonest or unjust, these words tend to pile up points against it in a way which may be quite out of proportion to the other evidence for its merits or demerits. Particularly awkward is the position of the man who wishes to deny the principle as a whole; for he still has to make use of the words in which the principle is expressed, which carry moral implications whether he likes it or not: so that he often finds himself having to make statements which in common usage are virtual contradictions, such as 'Justice is vice and folly' or 'Property is theft'. Usually the temptation to try to distort the empirical meaning of the words whilst retaining their moral implications is overwhelming: hence the perpetual concern with 'true justice', 'true patriotism', and so on.

Besides acting as reminders or *prima facie* reasons, moral principles as expressed in the limited words under discussion have the additional function, less commonly noted, of simply describing our moral judgements, as opposed to giving reasons for them or guiding us in making them. To talk of 'stealing' or 'injustice' describes in a single word a whole set of possible actions which I have morally judged or prejudged in a certain way. If I were asked by someone whose moral background and social culture were widely different from my own what my morality consisted of, I could most easily describe it by listing a number of rules (the Ten Commandments, for instance); and these rules would be expressed in limited words like 'stealing', 'coveting', 'adultery', 'lying' and so on. Indeed it is obviously essential that I should use limited words and not open words like 'good', or 'ought', since the latter have no empirical connotations and consequently give my hearer no information. It would not be informative if I were to say 'I eschew evil and do good'. What he wants to know is what sets of actions, having the same empirical characteristics, I single out for *prima facie* moral condemnation or approval.

We can see from this that the function of moral principles is sociological as well as logical. To utter such principles in a social context is to remind people, as members of society, of *prima facie* logical reasons for acting in a certain way, and to give simple descriptions which summarise our moral judgements; they refer us to a background of behaviour or behaviour-patterns which are approved by the society in which the principles are current, and of which we ourselves are supposed to approve. It is chiefly for sociological reasons that so many moral rules are negative; for the chief interest of society lies not so much in promoting moral excellence as in suppressing individual desires which are harmful to the community. (The existence of a law or prohibition implies that there are people who would act otherwise unless prohibited.) This descriptive function does, of course, have rational value in that a moral principle saves us the trouble of having to consider each case separately and on its own merits.

What philosophers and non-philosophers alike should remember, however, is that this value is neither more nor less than the value of any other general principle, and depends on how probable it is that any particular case can be subsumed under the principle. If we thought that in only 50 per cent of cases was it wrong to take what legally belonged to another, there would be no point in having a moral rule against stealing. In this respect the tendency of post-Kantian philosophers to say that moral principles can be 'universalised', or that only 'universal' principles can count as moral, is highly misleading. Any principle can be regarded as universal in the sense we have described, namely that we can remind ourselves of it in order to give ourselves a *prima facie* approximation of what is the right course of action; just as it is a *prima facie* point against a chess-player that his sacrificing the queen is unorthodox, against a man lighting a fire that he has placed the paper above the firewood, against a man starting a car that he presses the self-starter before taking it out of gear, and so on. No principle (unless it is a tautology, in which case we could hardly call it a principle) is universal in the sense that there are no exceptions to it, or that we could not conceive of exceptions to it. Universality is not a distinguishing mark of moral principles, and the temptation to ascribe to them some absolute or magical force which other principles lack must be resisted. As guides in cases of serious doubt they are virtually useless, and certainly not self-guaranteeing. Their function is the humbler but equally useful one which we have described.

(d) *Justice, Reward and Punishment*

The words 'just' and 'justice' are commonly used in our moral and political arguments. But it is unusual for anyone except a philosopher to enquire into the meanings of such words; and it is very unusual indeed for anyone (even a philosopher) to challenge their usefulness in helping us to solve our moral and political problems. From Plato onwards, philosophers have assumed, as all other people have assumed, that justice is of great importance: that the concept of justice is something which we cannot do without. This is a natural assumption, since 'just' is after all a word of praise, and one which is universally used. But I think the assumption is incorrect. For any value which the concept of justice may have in our moral thinking must depend on our wishing to praise or commend those actions, behaviour-patterns, or people to whom the purely descriptive sense of 'just' can properly refer. For 'just', of course, possesses both a descriptive and an evaluative significance: and the use of the word depends on our wishing to commend or value what it describes. But if we consider the descriptive meaning attentively enough, it seems to me doubtful whether we shall want to continue to make such wide use of 'just' as a word of praise at all. More briefly: if only actions or people that have the factual characteristics x, y, z can count as 'just', and if we do not generally wish to commend x, y, z, nor to disapprove of them, then 'just' is of little use to us as a moral word.

Many philosophers have attempted to analyse at least some uses of 'just', in terms of existing moral and legal codes; and this is supported by the first meaning given for 'just' in many reliable dictionaries, which is 'lawful' or 'law-abiding'. According to this analysis, we describe a verdict given by a judge as 'just', if it is in accordance with the law; and similarly an action can be described as 'just', if it is in accordance with a commonly accepted moral rule. But this cannot be a sufficient condition for justice, since we would not wish to describe a wicked man as 'just' even if he acted in a law-abiding manner; nor would we call every man 'just' who acted in accordance with accepted moral standards. This means only that we do not always accept laws or moral standards as good, and that 'just' has an evaluative implication as well as a descriptive meaning. Nor can this be a necessary condition; for we might wish to describe certain actions as 'just' even if they were contrary to the law and the accepted moral standards of the community in which they occurred. For instance, if a husband were to revenge the killing of his wife by himself killing the murderer, this might be against the law and the moral code of the community; but we might perfectly well call it 'just'. There is nothing to stop us disapproving of the law and the moral code, and thus calling actions 'just' which are either forbidden by law and morality, or are legally and morally neutral. Moreover, we might call such an action 'just' even if we approved of the law and the moral code; for though 'just' is a word of praise, it is still sense to say of an action that it was just but wrong, or that a man acted justly but that he ought not to have acted as he did.

We do, of course, frequently make use of the concept of justice in reference to laws and rules which are current in a community; but though there is a sociological connection between the two, there is no logical connection. Most of our laws and rules—or so we like to think—are made in order to satisfy the demands of justice; and hence we do in fact frequently describe law-abiding or moral actions as 'just'. But in an important sense they are only 'just' *per accidens*, and we would only call them so if they satisfied the true criteria for justice. The fact that many laws and rules embody these criteria is logically irrelevant. We may

95

say, if we wish, that the concept of justice implies the existence of some kind of 'moral law'. But in so far as it is helpful at all to say this, it means only that we wish to commend actions which have certain empirical characteristics.

The empirical characteristics of 'just' actions and people, as Aristotle first saw, are that they satisfy the principle of retribution or requital. A 'just' action is one which requites good with good (or pleasure with pleasure), and evil with evil (or pain with pain). Justice consists in rewarding people according to their 'deserts' or 'merits': and the deserts or merits of a man can be empirically verified at least to the extent of our being able to say whether (according to our moral standards) he is a good man or has done a beneficial action, in which case he 'deserves a reward', or is a bad man or has done harm, in which case he 'deserves to be punished'. Punishment is only just if the man punished has done wrong: otherwise it is not (except in a metaphorical sense) punishment at all, but ill-treatment or victimisation. Similarly we can only speak of a reward *of* or *for* some beneficent or right action. One cannot (logically) be rewarded for nothing: what one would receive would be merely a piece of good fortune. Imagine two cases: (1) A man deliberately commits a foul and cold-blooded murder. Although he is sane by any normal definition of sanity, it is agreed that the best treatment for him would be to give him a long and comfortable holiday with pay; and the judge, who is legally empowered to order this, does so order. (2) A man is associated with a gang of thieves, whom through ignorance he believes to be law-abiding citizens; nor has he himself acted wrongly in any moral sense. It is agreed that to imprison or execute him would have an excellent deterrent effect upon actual criminals; and this decision, which we will suppose to be legally admissible, is put into effect. Now although both actions or types of treatment are legal, and though we might agree that both were generally beneficial, we could not possibly describe them as 'just'. For, we would say, neither man 'deserves' such treatment. The former does not deserve anything pleasant, and the latter does not deserve anything unpleasant. And our sole reason for saying this is that the former has acted wrongly, and that the latter has not.

But this descriptive criterion for justice is not yet complete. To act justly, we must not only requite good for good and evil for evil; we must also do so in some kind of proportion. A very good action deserves a high reward; a less meritorious one, a lesser reward; and similarly with punishment. This proportion is basically conceived in terms of equality, as expressed in 'An eye for an eye, a tooth for a tooth'; or in the line quoted by Aristotle, 'If he suffers what he has made another suffer, then true justice is done'. But usually the matter is more complex than that. What a man deserves is not always decided by discovering what he has done, and then doing the same to him; or in other words, the *merit* of an action is not always decided simply by reference to the action itself. We consider also the man's intentions and motives, his character and the circumstances of his case. Thus we might fine a man £50 for stealing £5, or punish him with death for attempted murder. Here we are requiting, not the action itself, but the intentions behind the action. The wickedness of stealing and attempted murder is not lessened because the theft was only of £5, or because the murder did not come off. Similarly, we might give a man a medal for conspicuous bravery and good service, though the medal would not be worth as much to him as his bravery and good service were worth to the community. The scale of merit and demerit which we adopt is largely dictated by social and moral considerations, and is not usually so crude as the *lex talionis*. But there is always a scale: and for an award to be just it must conform to the scale. Thus to punish stealing more harshly than murder, or to reward a man of average bravery with a higher decoration than an outstandingly brave man, would be unjust. We also call such treatment 'unfair': and fairness, like justice, is not completely tied down to equality, but rather to whatever scale of awards is accepted in a community.

There is also another way in which the concept of equality assists in the application of justice, to which we refer when we use words like 'equitable' or 'impartial'. If we are distributing prizes or punishments for something which those who receive them have done, we consider the merits and demerits of the people concerned. This retributive—or requital—use of things, whether good things for prizes or bad things for punishments, influences us also when we are merely distributing things without any prior reference to merit or demerit at all. Thus if we are called upon to distribute a number of sweets to some children, not as prizes but simply as pleasures, our distribution is nevertheless affected by the fact that we often do regard pleasant things like sweets as prizes. The reason why, if there are *n* children and *n* sweets, we think that (other things being equal) each child should receive one sweet and one only, is simply that (other things being equal) we think that no child deserves more than another. So far as this particular distribution is concerned, all the children have equal merit. Other things are not equal when one or more children has done some particularly good or bad action which is outstanding, in the sense that it has not been requited. For then the merits of the children are not equal: then we say 'You don't deserve a sweet because you've been a bad boy', or 'You deserve an extra sweet, because you've been a good boy'. In other words, we tend to regard pains and pleasures as punishments and rewards whenever possible: we keep an eye permanently open for the chance of satisfying the retributive principle. And the important part played by impartiality, equity or equality in justice derives from the fact that retribution is often best satisfied—or at least not vitiated—by an equal distribution.

It should be noticed that justice cannot be fully described in terms of rewards, punishments and equity of distribution. Yet wherever it cannot be so described, it still remains clear that the notion of repayment and requital is basic. Examples of this are to be found in the repayment of obligations. Thus we may say: 'Your parents looked after you when you were young: it's only just that you should look after them when they are old'; or 'Your country has done a lot for you: it's only fair that you should help to defend it in time of need'. The just man is the man who tends to live up to the principle of retribution.

As I have suggested, it seems doubtful to what extent we really believe in the value of retribution either as a means to an end, or as an end in itself. I suggest, however, that far more people consider retribution to be a good thing in itself than most philosophers, who are perhaps more than usually enlightened, tend to imagine. There is some linguistic evidence for this. The statement 'He deserves to be hanged', for instance, actually means 'It is in accordance with the principle of retribution that he should be hanged'; but it is always used to imply, and often to entail, 'He ought to be hanged'. Remarks of this kind are very common; and they seem to show that most people do not wish to look further than the principle of retribution for a justification of their treatment of criminals or benefactors. To most people, it is self-evident that wrongdoers ought to be punished, whether or not their punishment is effective as a deterrent or a reformative influence; and similarly it is generally believed that virtue should be rewarded, irrespective of whether or not it encourages men to be more virtuous. The view that our belief in retribution is rational, in the sense that most people would defend it by reference to higher moral criteria or more exalted ends, seems to me psychologically naïve. There are excellent psychological reasons for believing that it is far more deeply engrained than that.[1]

Nevertheless, a closer inspection of our actual application of the concept of justice in the world of practical affairs would, I think, tend to devalue justice in the eyes of many. This is particularly true in reference to punishment, which merits closer attention. Let us first be clear that if we did not believe in giving pain or causing unpleasantness to those who have done wrong, as a good thing in itself, we could quite well do without the word 'punishment' altogether. As we can see from certain metaphorical usages, for instance when we say that a boxer is 'taking plenty of punishment', anything which is to count as punishment must be painful or unpleasant. Moreover, it must be retributive; that is to say, we would not call painful treatment meted out to an innocent person 'punishment', however valuable the deterrent effects on other members

[1] Cf. J. C. Flugel, *Man, Morals and Society* (Pelican edition, 1955), ch. 11.

of society might be. In other words, if we approve of punishment, we approve of inflicting pain on certain people as an end in itself. For if we approved of inflicting pain solely on the grounds that it acted as an effective reformative influence, we should not need to talk of punishment at all. We should be able to talk merely of 'treatment'. Some people, from humanitarian or other motives, do in fact consider how we ought to treat evildoers without reference to retribution at all: and to these people 'punishment' is an otiose word, adding nothing but confusion to their thinking.

I do not think that all those who profess a belief in retribution would be prepared to defend the infliction of pain, even upon evildoers, as an end in itself. What misleads them, I think, is the notion that the infliction of pain must, in some curious way, be right when it is inflicted upon those who are morally at fault. Thus, if a man is foolish enough to touch an exposed electric wire, he gets a painful shock; and this shock is effective both as a deterrent and as a reformative influence for his folly. But folly is not (in this case at least) a moral fault, and the pain is not deliberately administered by human agency; and for those reasons we would not call the shock 'punishment'. Nor would we necessarily think that the pain was good as an end in itself; we might quite well think that there were better ways of teaching him not to touch exposed electric wires. Only moral errors can (logically) be punished; and in these cases we seem to believe, either that the infliction of pain is good in itself, or that pain alone can act as an effective deterrent or reformative influence. Neither of these beliefs seems to be rational. For those who believe in pain as an end in itself in such cases cannot give reasons why this belief should not be extended to cover the infliction of pain in cases which are not moral issues—an extension which only a confirmed sadist would wish to make: and those who believe that only pain, in moral cases, can effectively deter or reform commit themselves to a psychological generalisation for which there is, to say the least, not adequate evidence.

There is, moreover, a difficulty about punishment, and indeed retribution in general, which has not been sufficiently observed. We can (logically) only punish or requite those who act freely: and certainly we would think ourselves greatly in error if we meted out punishment-treatment to a man who had not acted freely. But, as I have explained previously, the criterion of free action consists in determining whether the cause for the action is 'inside' the man, or 'outside' him: if it is an internal cause, we say he acted freely (using 'he' to include the cause), if external we say he was compelled (using 'he' to exclude the cause). More often than not we do not know the causes of men's actions; and hence we are not able to say whether they acted freely or not. In these cases, we should not know whether they ought to receive punishment-treatment. Yet in fact we frequently punish people without knowing the causes for their actions; and sometimes we regret it, as we regret having 'punished' people whom we now know to be kleptomaniacs rather than thieves. This seems to make the notion of punishment to apply in practice.

Nor are our notions of reward and punishment consistent. It is commonly held, for example, that those who are more intelligent or gifted than their fellows 'deserve' to receive a greater 'reward' for their labour; and this, in practice and in theory, entails that those who are less intelligent and gifted receive a lesser reward. These latter may possess as much moral virtue as the former: they may be as diligent, loyal, industrious, etc., but their 'merits', when we are considering the distribution of wealth, are not held to be so great. It seems clear, from the language in which these views are expressed, that we are prepared to apply the principle of retribution to more than moral issues; for in general we believe that a man is not responsible for his intelligence or his gifts, but only for the way in which he uses them. In this sort of case we cannot defend the retributive principle on the grounds that it is an effective incentive or deterrent, since you cannot increase intelligence, nor multiply talents, by praise or reward. And this tends to support the view, already mentioned, that the retributive principle is commonly regarded as an end in itself.

I do not think that many people who examine the concept of justice, and its cognate concepts of reward and punishment, with sufficient attention would still be prepared to include them in their ultimate moral criteria. But this does not mean, of course, that we must necessarily adopt a violently humanitarian attitude towards the criminal law, nor does it mean that the structure of the law will collapse. For we can perfectly well make a moral assessment of any citizen in reference to the law, and treat him in whatever way is best for him and society, without considerations of justice at all; and moreover such treatment may well have to be painful, in many cases, if it is to be effective. Nor, again, does the abandonment of justice involve us in political egalitarianism: a view which, as I hope to have shown, is itself only a watered-down version of justice. For it may well be true that reward according to merit is an effective incentive to harder work or more efficient performances. But it should be stressed that our only evidence for this must be empirical; and such facts as psychologists and sociologists have revealed seem to suggest that the views of the layman on these questions are by no means obviously correct. We must proceed with caution.

4. THE USES OF MORALISM

To the Moralist the situation now appears rather like the end of *Brave New World*: all the concepts which have hitherto formed the armour of human dignity are now devalued, chopped up, made hygienic, sterilised, whisked away. Whisk, freedom: whisk, morality and moral principles: whisk, whisk, justice, reward and punishment.... The Moralist wants to cry out 'No!', or say something like 'If that's where logic leads you, give me the decent feelings of the ordinary chap', or (if he is sophisticated) turn to existentialism or the Catholic Church. More probably, he will hardly bother to listen to us. As ordinary people have always done, he will continue to use precisely the same moral concepts as he has always done: and he will be right, in a way, because so far we have done nothing for him at all.

In a way, too, we have made a false contrast. We have led people to think that there are two modes of moral thinking, and only two. Either you are a utilitarian or a Kantian, either an expediency-merchant or an intuitionist, either Factualist or a Moralist. But throughout we have been concerned, really, with only one sort of language-situation. We have been concerned with doubt, with people not knowing how to think, discussing, arguing, ratiocinating, trying to *work out* things. We have been weighing the logic and the use of concepts from this point of view only: and it is not at all odd that Factualism seems to have had things all its own way, since it is precisely this sort of situation which it is designed to suit. We have considered the human tribe only when it meets to debate. But, of course, it meets for all sorts of other purposes: to dance, to pray, to sit in judgement, to punish, to educate, and so forth. What we have described by the very short-hand of 'Moralism' may, in fact, have hundreds of uses—almost as many uses as there are language-situations.

One can easily fall, almost without noticing it, into the mistake of supposing that the philosopher's business begins and ends with the one language-situation for which Factualism is eminently suited—the situation of discussion and ratiocination. This derives from the fallacy that it is only when people are working things out that they are acting or talking rationally—that to be reasonable means to be ratiocinating. But we have only to state this to see through it.

There are times when you work things out, and times when you act: and there are plenty of other times in addition to these. When an employee does something wrong, you can do various things: reason with him, use moral persuasion on him, hit him, denounce him to the boss, and so forth. All these, in different contexts, may be rational. It is the philosopher's business, not only to assist with contexts of ratiocination, but also to clarify and explain the logic of other quite different contexts: to show what it is that the tribe is doing, as it were, when it sits in judgement, prays, dances, and so on.

Nor is this mistake confined to philosophers. We talk of 'moral arguments' or 'political discussions': but on the vast majority of occasions when people get together and use moral language, argument and discussion (in the sense of ratiocination) play a very small part. You can do hundreds of things with moral concepts besides *argue* with

105

them: you can complain, praise, bully, cajole, exhort, inspire, condemn, educate, win votes, and so forth. Many people think they are discussing, when in fact they are doing something else. I have a neighbour who occupies some twenty minutes of my time each day in 'discussing', as she would put it, the difficulties of her job. But if I ask myself, *à la* Wittgenstein, what language-game she is playing, it is plain that she is not giving an outline of empirical facts, or suggesting improvements in the régime under which she lives, or expressing doubt about anything. She is complaining, asking for sympathy, getting my support as another member of the tribe. Yet even in such a case there is nothing irrational about her language-game:[1] it is a game which the difficulties of life and the need for tribal sympathy compel us all to play.

Most moral contexts of language are more like this than they are like the examples of 'moral discussions' which occasionally find their way into philosophical text-books, and which look unreal and jejune precisely because non-ratiocinative contexts are omitted. Of course there is no reason why philosophers must always be true to life in this way, any more than a dramatist has to clutter up his play with the light, meaningless chit-chat in which real people indulge. But they must be aware of the variety of language-situations. It is *people* who use language: language is something that serves human purposes. It is not enough to have a few catchwords with which we can casually write off non-ratiocinative language:

---

[1] In talking of 'language-games' or just 'games' I make use of a convenient piece of contemporary philosophers' jargon. As the present context shows, it is not intended that these 'games' should not be taken seriously. One might talk of 'language-uses' or 'language-situations'. Some points connected with the idea of language as a set of games are discussed on pp. 174–7.

'emotive', 'persuasive', 'ritualistic', 'performatory'. This is like taking the tribe seriously when it is doing the things we understand, like debating or praying, and writing off the rest as 'ritual'.

It is difficult to do any sort of justice to the rich variety of moral purposes in which Moralism plays a part. Here again it is wisest, if less tidy, to begin by listing some scattered points.

(1) Moralism can reinforce a context of discussion, and thus contribute to ratiocination. Thus, we have seen[1] that the quotation of a moral principle ('But that's stealing') makes a useful *prima facie* point against a certain action which might be under discussion.

(2) The Moralist may be directing attention to long-term consequences which escape the impatient Factualist: for instance, the extent to which theft or untruthfulness weaken the social system, or (more subtly) the extent to which the practice of such vices may promote discord or unhappiness in the mind of the individual who contemplates them.

(3) He may be rejecting the whole *tone* of a discussion in Factualism whereby the correct moral action appears as the end result of a calculation: he may be, in effect, begging or warning those occupied in discussion to *feel* more, to take the whole thing more seriously. The Factualist appears to the Moralist as irresponsible, not feeling the weight of morality heavily enough, not bearing the communal burden. The Moralist uses his language (perhaps unconsciously) to bring home the importance of the subject. In this context, such talk would make the Factualist more cautious, less likely to overlook important facts, less casual.

(4) The Moralist may be operating as an educationalist.

[1] See pp. 88–93.

Thus, his moral language may be partly addressed to himself, to keep himself up to the moral mark, as it were, to remind himself of the importance of his moral concepts, to prevent himself being carried away both at the time and on future occasions, by his desires or his foolish passions. Or it may be addressed to his fellows for similar purposes: not to make them less casual (so that they will not overlook the facts), but as a warning addressed to the person as a whole (not merely to the person ratiocinating in that particular context). He is speaking, as it were, to his own or his neighbour's *soul*, to the whole personality. Or he may be disowning him, both condemning and making it clear that he himself wants no part of his viewpoint or his personality—as one might do, say, in expelling a schoolboy.

(5) He may be applying praise and blame as one might apply pleasure and pain, simply for the very good Factualist reason that the human machine he is talking to will work better after the application—as one might oil a bicycle: in psychological terms, perhaps, trying to strengthen the man's super-ego: in religious terms, appealing to his conscience. Or he might be, not so much adjusting the machine as instructing it: much as scientists 'programme' computing machines, or as one might 'give instructions', so to speak, to the auto-pilot in an aeroplane. This has an obvious use, for example, in bringing up children, when one tries to build in certain values; to graft them on to the child's personality, to 'programme' the child to act in certain ways.

(6) He might be acting as a sociologist or a politician: it is in such contexts, for instance, that remarks like 'if everyone did that there would be social chaos' are best understood. He might say that Factualism was not

capable of being successfully followed by the mass of people, because they are too stupid or too selfish, and therefore that it should not be promulgated.

(7) He may be asking us to remember an *alternative view of human beings*. The Factualist asks us to consider them as machines: his rival asks us to consider them as 'moral agents', 'souls', 'real people'. To call this purpose of language 'sociological' is to devalue it unnecessarily: it is more correct, if less cosy, to call it 'spiritual'. The Moralist is here complaining of his rival's lack of warmth, love, sympathy, appreciation of what is human dignity, human right, and the need to treat men as ends in themselves and not as bits of machinery. His protest against the machine thesis, in this context, will be that there are other equally important theses: that men are *men*, and not (when all is said and done) machines in the usual sense. For 'machine' in this sense implies something made for human purposes, to serve man and be adjusted by him to suit his own ends. This is like saying 'Look at the cathedral as a cathedral: never mind what you can *do* with it, how you can exploit it scientifically: value it, treat it with respect—treat it almost like a person. Take it seriously.'

These are brief, almost perfunctory sketches, but they should be sufficient to give us some idea of what the Moralist may be getting at. Can we say of any one of these sketches that this is what he is *really* getting at? We hardly know how to answer this, since people do not consciously adopt a language-game for a deliberate and predesignated purpose: and at the same time it is plain that Moralist concepts do, in fact, enter usefully into all the language-contexts in all the sketches. And if we say that the 'spirit' of Moralism conflicts with the 'spirit' of Factualism in certain contexts but not in others, we shall be in danger of a highly subjective interpretation of what this 'spirit' is, in either case. What we can do, however, is to see how much trouble is required to square Moralism with Factualism in various contexts: and this may give us some reasonable grounds for maintaining that Moralism is more fundamental in some contexts than in others.

Thus, where the Moralist is speaking to reinforce the context of discussion, or from an educational or political standpoint, a Factualist would say that his rival is merely helping him to do his job: and hence that his rival's concepts are 'really' part of Factualism. Directing attention to long-term consequences, commenting on the political or educational effects of certain actions or the promulgation of certain principles, making people take morality seriously, improving them by praise or blame— all this, it might be said, is merely to practise Factualism in a wide context. The considerations here all fit quite comfortably into an utilitarian pattern. Such a view gains support from the tendency of the average Moralist to support his principles by utilitarian arguments. For instance, if I query the importance of retributive justice, I shall at once be told that this query must not be upheld because there would be more crime and less hard work if it were: and if I argue for divorce by consent, I shall be told not only that it would be against the will of God, but also that it would produce social chaos.

However, if one attends to moral contexts in real life, one cannot avoid the impression that the Moralist does not really want to play the Factualist's game in this way. He begins, nearly always, by trying to settle the discussion by the mere weight, as it were, of his moral concepts: by flashing the aegis of Justice, to dazzle and overwhelm his opponent. Thus, if we are debating the value of compulsory religion or compulsory games at a school, it is plain that their defendants prefer, if possible, to regard these institutions as good in themselves. But remarks emerge, such as 'It is good for boys to do something they don't like doing', or 'Discipline is a good thing in itself', which suggest somehow that the very questioning of the institutions has already initiated the process of degeneration. When pressed—but only when pressed—the defendants will begin to use utilitarian arguments, like 'The school would go to pieces without religion', or 'Organised games keep the boys out of mischief', or 'The parents wouldn't like religion done away with'. Arguments of this type are often sound, and point to real and important sociological factors which the average liberally-minded and unrealistic Factualist would overlook. But the Moralist does not *like* using them.

Very well, what *does* the Moralist want to do? We have found a use for his concepts, as an addition to Factualism: but it is not the use he wants. If we consider the social effects of the use of his concepts, we may get some clue. When they are arrayed in full force and deployed against the Factualist, the latter is made to feel irresponsible, dishonest, untrustworthy, *disloyal*. Disloyalty is the overall charge which the Moralist makes. His opponent is disloyal to authority and the community: the community's moral concepts are not good enough for him: he wants to change things, to undermine social values, to question and to criticise. It is as if the Moralist were speaking as an elder of the tribe, stopping the young men from getting into evil ways or from upsetting tradition: or as if we should all consider ourselves as children beneath the fatherly guidance and imperatives of the moral law, the established morality.

(The closeness of Moralism with religion, especially patriarchal religion, here becomes obvious.) The Moralist uses his concepts to appeal to our consciences, to that part of us which has been formed and indoctrinated by our parents, our pastors and masters, and which is *a priori* on the side of established morality. He is saying, in effect, 'Obey!' It is no accident that the Moralist is usually found among the right-wing, conservative, forces of law and order, and on the side of established religion: or that his rival tends towards tender or tough-minded liberalism or radicalism, and sides with the forces of change.

However, this is not always the case: and we must beware of tying down language-games too closely to specific sociological functions. The Moralist does not have to be on the side of his community: though he does have to be committed to some moral feeling or principle which is not simply the result of calculation and rational choice. Thus, most pacifists ('*conscientious* objectors') follow Moralism: that is, their pacifism is usually not the end product of a utilitarian sum, but arises from some strongly felt moral principle which they feel to be binding upon them. They do not say 'By refusing to fight I shall be achieving the best possible state of affairs all round': they say 'I must not fight', or 'It is wrong for me to fight'. Of course 'I must not fight' *might* be the end product of a calculation: perhaps for some pacifists it is. But for most it is a matter of conscience, an imperative: not a case where one weighs the various factors—the educational value of pacifist example on the community, the actual effect a refusal to fight will have upon the amount of killing that gets done, and so forth. Yet, despite his Moralist methods, the pacifist is of course in general opposition to his community, and merits the charge of 'disloyal' as much as any Factualist.

Nevertheless, there is still a sense in which the Moralist who forms part of a minority group is less disloyal than the Factualist. The community will think 'at least he *has* moral principles, and perhaps his motives are sound; at least he recognises *some* authority': whereas the Factualist is disloyal in principle, so to speak, since his game is based on doubt, the existence of problems, and the need for working things out. If the Factualist is one of a tribe, it is a tribe of scientists or committee-men: but even the minority-group Moralist feels himself to be, at least potentially, a member of a tribe bound by a common morality, common indignation, and common ideals. The ideals may seem rather esoteric to the rest of the community, to the majority that surrounds him: but they are none the less potent for him and in him. He is still playing the Moralist game: it is merely that his rules and scoring system, so to speak, may be the inverse of other rules and systems. He still wants to talk about disloyalty, honesty, conscience, and so on: he still wants to use his moral weight, to apply moral *pressure*.

This indicates a language-game which has nothing to do with the practice of Factualism—even though it may be justified by Factualism. We can clarify the point by observing the Moralist's reaction to the men-as-machines view again. If men are machines, at least their behaviour suggests that they are cybernetic or self-regulating machines. They can 'programme' themselves. They are conscious. Thus, we do not *have* to regard them scientifically, in the sense that we must spread out their blue-prints on the table and see what has gone wrong. We can often make them go right by just talking to them (like an ingenious toy motor-car I once had, which went when you said 'Go!' to it): or they can go right by themselves, improve themselves by their own increased awareness and determination (this motor-car stopped ten seconds after you had said 'Go!', and used to engage a lower gear if it came to an upward slope). But, now, supposing a very clever scientist comes along, who can make anyone go right without talking to him at all, without regarding him as a solid human being, simply by spreading out his blue-print and then using a screwdriver in the right places. Suppose, to make it more concrete, we find we can produce virtuous action by adjusting the brain-cells with scalpels, electric charges, and so forth. Suppose, in fact, we find that it is just this adjustment of brain-cells which all the talk of education, upbringing, moralising, praising, blaming, etc. actually achieves, and that we can now short-cut it by direct action. What does the Moralist say now?

He does *not* regard this as entirely satisfactory: and this shows that his language-purposes cannot be easily squared with Factualism; that they cannot be regarded either as an addition to it, or as a clumsy version of it. He wants to be able to address the man-machine as a solid human being: to say 'You are wrong', not merely 'You have gone wrong'. We could put this unkindly by saying that he really wants there to be a little man inside the human being, a little man who is not at all a machine and whom he can, therefore, address in the terms he wishes to use. Or we could put it more kindly, by saying that he wants a holistic rather than an analytic view of a human being. The Moralist insists on an alternative view, opposed to the machine view. He wants a human being to be regarded as a *person*. Not really an unreasonable point of view, we might think.

We can now see the two halves of what I take to be the most (apparently) serious conflict. It is much like the old worry about the possibility of a satisfying relationship with anyone or anything if we also have an analytic approach. 'How can I love her if I regard her every act as a product of psychological motivations?' would be a typical expression of such anxiety. But we ought to know, in this case, that the worry is unnecessary. We might say 'How can I love nature if I know how it works by studying biology?', and this is obviously silly: in fact, it is usually just those people who know about plants and animals who also love them and find satisfaction in contemplating and being with them. We can now say, quite simply, that each half of the conflict can be satisfied, provided it does not try to claim the rights of a whole. You can be analytic at one time, and holistic at another. The fact that we can regard men as machines does not preclude our regarding them as 'living, breathing human beings', with human dignity and human rights.

We can, of course, discuss the further question of when we ought to take a Moralist view and when we ought to take a Factualist view, or of how far we ought to take either view. This is asking, when ought we to condemn, moralise, remind people of authority, social values and the humanity of the individual, and when ought we to calculate, work things out, and consider the mechanism of the individual? Or how much should each aspect occupy our minds? The fact that we should settle this question, or work it out, by Factualist methods is no more than a verbal point in favour of Factualism: settling questions and working things out is what the Factualist does. But it is an important point. When we want to work things out, we must not become involved in doing something else. We cannot profitably discuss the general use of morality, or its particular applications, by moralising.

Unless we grasp this fully, we shall not be able to resist the tendency to thorough-going irrationalism which the Moralist sometimes uses as his last line of defence.

But then, he should not be driven back to this line of defence. Nowadays the Factualist has it all his own way: science is at a premium, psychology has advanced, the very existence of 'thinking machines' virtually scores a point for his side. Already it *sounds* quite alright to say that a table is 'really' just atoms and void: there seems little hope of getting people to see it as a work of art; or as an object which really exists in its own right (and is not merely something to be used or exploited); or even—so great is the power of science—as an ordinary table. To ask people to lay stress on a personal approach to other people sounds reactionary in an age of psychology: to ask them to lay stress on a personal or semi-personal approach to physical objects sounds absurdly anthropomorphic in an age of science. But both demands might be not only reasonable but vital: and the Moralist might well claim that the advance of science, ending up with the men-as-machines thesis, has only been made at the price of losing the capability of taking other viewpoints.

Do these viewpoints matter? Why *not* just exploit things and people? We now reach the ultimate point, when we have cashed out the language of the Moralist into the currency of human purposes. Of course purposes can be more or less sane and sensible, but it is difficult to judge them without far wider experience than most of us possess. Certain things are obvious. For instance, satisfaction and sanity depend to a great extent on human relationships: human relationships, if they are to be successful, depend upon our being able to see people as *solid*, not merely as blue-prints: so that a holistic approach to personality plainly expresses and satisfies a sane and sensible purpose. What about a non-analytic approach to works of art or the physical world—to nature, for instance? There may be sane people who do not 'appreciate' (i.e. respond holistically to) works of art or to nature, just as there may be sane people who see human beings merely as blue-prints; though one doubts it. (Probably there is a sliding scale, and people are more or less adept at a holistic approach to these various things.) But at the very least, one would want to say that they were missing something.

Yet this is hardly strong enough. A religious believer would say that an unbeliever was missing something by not being able to respond to the divinity, both immanent in the world and transcending it. He might add that the unbeliever could 'get by' without such a response. But then—can he really 'get by'? How *much* does he miss? Perhaps more than he thinks. On the other hand, the unbeliever might say that the believer is not responding to anything at all, making the obvious logical point that the use of the word 'responding' implies that there is really something to respond to. The believer may be merely investing the world with divinity; his god may be a projection; he may not be treating the world and its features for what it is. Similarly, not *every* non-machine view of human beings is necessarily desirable, or necessarily satisfies sensible human purposes. We can view a man holistically and wisely, because he is a man: but sometimes he can be an object of terror to us (perhaps because he is a policeman): or he can be an object of romantic obsession (if one is neurotically in love with him): and so on. Similarly again, we can respond properly to Chopin: or we can invest his music with nostalgia and sentiment, because we associate it with an adolescent love-affair.

But this is no more than a preliminary sketch: and the chief point to be made before we try to enlarge it is that the mere clarification of what purpose and language-game we are pursuing in any one context (if philosophers could only help people to be aware of this) would be of considerable value in itself. At least it would shift the discussion to a higher level: the people concerned could then discuss the wisdom of these purposes, instead of merely playing different games on the same board.

We can try to go some way in discussing the wisdom of Moralist purposes: but first it is necessary to sum up briefly the points made above. It emerges from them that Moralism fulfils two main purposes:

(1) What we may call sociological purposes: calling attention to authority, reinforcing morality, educating, persuading, changing the human machine and 'programming' it, acting as the guardian of law and order, and so forth.

(2) What we may call spiritual purposes: reminding us of the importance of a holistic view of personality, of the solidity of human beings, of the soul.

Now it could truly be said of the *moral*, concepts of Moralism (and here I exclude notions like 'freedom', 'the self', 'the soul' and so on) that they are not used primarily for spiritual purposes, but only for sociological ones. This is to say, the whole game which the Moralist plays with words such as 'blame', 'stealing', 'wicked' and so on is not intended to remind us of the importance of the holistic view, nor are its rules dictated with this in mind. The existence of the game may imply such a view: that is, we *might* quote the importance of the view as a good reason for playing the game. We might say that the game itself is not a spiritual game, but a sociological one. In playing it, the Moralist is not actually reminding us of the soul: he is reinforcing morality, educating, persuading, etc. On the other hand, Moralist notions like 'free will', 'the self' and 'the soul', though they may indeed have useful sociological consequences, seem capable of being used in a different game. This game represents a way of looking at human beings, almost a way of describing them; it is different from the mechanistic way of looking at them and describing them, and even more different from the socio-logical game (played with moral concepts) which is designed to educate and persuade them, to buttress their morality.

In order to give the discussion a little more precision, we can now profitably introduce a distinction between:

(*a*) The *usage* of a particular moral concept, that is, its place in a particular language-game, the way in which its grammar and logic work.

(*b*) The *use* of the concept and of the language-game of which it is a part, that is, whether the game is a game of fact-stating, persuasion, judging, etc.

(*c*) The *usefulness* of the concept and of the game, that is, whether the purposes it is supposed to fulfil are sensible, and whether also it actually fulfils these purposes.

It is important to make this logical fuss about use and usage and usefulness, because there is a standing temptation among philosophers to suppose that to have established and clarified one of these is to have established and clarified the others: in particular, to suppose that to have shown the use of a game is to have shown its useful-ness. But this is plainly not so. Thus, we might say that the *use* of hockey is to give organised occupation, of such-and-such a kind, and with such-and-such rules, to twenty-two people: that is the sort of game it is. But we might prefer to decide its *usefulness* by considering, for example, how much exercise it gave to growing boys, or whether it inculcated team spirit. Or again, we might conceivably teach children how to do simple arithmetic by getting them to play a card-game: and here too we can describe the card-game adequately, but still reserve the right to say that it would be more profitable for them to learn their tables. We could say this, even if the game were designed as a teaching game (not merely as a game of cards): we could say that the use of the game was to teach, but that it was not particularly useful for this purpose—or not as useful as learning tables.

Do Moralist games do whatever jobs they are supposed to do, and are these jobs good jobs? Here there is a temptation to accept the games: first, because their jobs are obviously good, and secondly, because no other games seem to do them. This is particularly true of the second type of game, whose objective is to insist on the solidity of human beings, on human souls. Thus J. R. Lucas in an essay on 'The Soul' writes:[1] 'If we do not believe that people have souls then we shall not do by them as we would be done by, except in so far as expediency dictates; we shall not hesitate to use them merely as means and not at all as ends...' and even puts in a good word for the religion-game: '...whoever believes in the existence of the Christian God must also believe in the existence and the value of his children... whoever does not believe in God will not believe in others either. Nor long believe even in himself alone.' This is very plausible, because we all *want* to believe in the existence and value of God's children: none of us *likes* being used as means and not as ends: we all want to use this language, and the idea that we shall not even be able

[1] *Faith and Logic*, ed. Basil Mitchell (Allen and Unwin, 1957), pp. 146–8.

to believe in ourselves, unless we play this language-game, is really frightening. No wonder so many people play it, we think. But then, perhaps, we think again. Aren't there other games which fulfil the same purposes just as well (the humanist game, for instance)? And just how well does the soul-game and the God-game actually do the job? Haven't the people who have played it in the past been just as liable to use people as means and not as ends— or more liable? And isn't this because the game leaves the question of how we view people far too open, and makes it far too easy for us to project our own desires into the game, to make up our own rules?

What we have to reject is the notion that the Factualist's language-game, his talk of men-as-machines, *necessarily* involves us in a wicked, totalitarian chess-game with human beings as pawns. Men may be like machines, but they are not *ipso facto* the less to be valued: indeed, perhaps the more we get to know about what makes them tick, the more we shall learn to love them. Further, there seems no reason why we should suppose that one machine is any more entitled to exploit another than one man is entitled to exploit another, or one of God's children is entitled to exploit another. The way in which the Moralist's spiritual game is played, in practice, does not *obviously* demonstrate that the game is necessary if we are to have a proper respect for human beings: and to add to it the religion-game does not help. For those who over-employ words like 'soul', 'responsibility' and 'free will' do not appear more obviously as liberators than those who over-employ words like 'super-ego', 'complex' and 'libido'. If there are Jesus and the Buddha, there are also Freud and Jung: and if there are wicked Factualist exploiters like Caesar and Stalin, there are also Moralist Grand Inquisitors.

What the men-as-machines view does do, however, is to make exploitation easier—as any increased human knowledge and power does. The ability of Factualism to establish publicly verifiable facts about human beings, by the use of psychological science, is at once its strength and its weakness: its strength, because what is publicly verifiable can be publicly agreed, and its weakness, because what is publicly agreed can be put into operation on the public. Backward countries have to use the primitive mechanisms of pleasure and pain, of justice, reward and punishment: civilised countries can use a more subtle psychology. In a backward country the possibilities of interference with the individual are less: there are laws, and if you break them and get caught you pay the penalty. This is a rap over the knuckles, not interference. In a civilised country, before very long, we may find ourselves taken away by smooth men in white coats who 'adjust' us: always of course, using publicly agreed methods. Nobody wants to be primitive, everyone wants to be scientific. We want to *help* the poor criminals. But we may be criminals ourselves some day, and somehow we distrust those smooth men in white coats.

So we need some view to supplement the machine view: and if the spiritual, holistic picture of Moralism can give it to us, without other disadvantages, good luck to it. But it is important that the view should be as positive and as realistic as possible. If we use it or interpret it (as too often happens) merely as a protest against Factualism, then it is not likely to last very long. First, a mere protest does not assist us in facing the very real problems of how to deal with people (not only criminals): it merely asks us to close our eyes to the psychological facts. Secondly, a protest does not offer us any alternative view which is based on reality: it gets dismissed as obscurantist or 'metaphysical' (in the pejorative way in which some philosophers use the word). Thirdly, and most important of all, it gives us nothing positive to back up the very good point that might otherwise be made about the importance of freedom.

Defenders of freedom in the liberal tradition of the western world are (very properly) opposed to what they call 'interference' or 'indoctrination'. The idea is that men are ends in themselves, that we must not bring *pressure* to bear on them. But, in the light of a realistic psychology, what is to count as pressure? We might say: other things can interfere besides rubber truncheons, and there are other methods of indoctrination besides brainwashing. In other words, it is not necessarily the most overt and obvious methods of compulsion which are the most compulsive. Suppose I am a schoolmaster, and a boy comes to me (or is brought to me) who is in some difficult situation. I can do various things: I can force him (by threats or actual violence) to take some particular course, I can use moral pressure on him, or half-hypnotise him, as it were, by being an authoritative, clean-limbed schoolmaster. All right, this is interference or indoctrination. But now, supposing I simply give him advice and know that he will take it because he likes and admires me? Is this not just as effective a method? It might be more effective. Or suppose I refuse to deal with him at all—surely in this case I can escape the charge of indoctrination? But no, it seems; I may know that if I do nothing he will take Blogg's advice, or be guided by the earlier injunctions of his parents. And then shall I not, in fact, have decided to let this happen to him, which means that I have decided to take a course which results in his doing such-and-such? And is that not just as much my doing as would be my persuading, or even forcing, him to do something else?

This is simply to say that everything one does, and everything one omits to do, does in fact affect other people. Obviously, in point of ordinary use, I am not interfering with a stranger in the street if I pass by on the other side, nor am I indoctrinating him, nor am I even influencing him. But then he is influenced by something else: and the responsibility for this (albeit in a weak sense) is mine. (It would be my responsibility in a very strong sense if he were wounded or needed help in any way.) Thus the defender of freedom, whether he is thinking on a political level or on the level of individual personal relationships, has to give some positive reason for objecting to those types of influence which we normally describe as 'interference' or 'indoctrination', and for accepting other types of influence. He cannot just say 'Hands off!', because there is an important sense in which we cannot keep our hands off, or at least in which, if we keep our hands off, somebody or something else will lay hands on.

The defender will naturally turn to the commonly accepted picture of an individual's 'inner self', or 'free will', and say that it is this 'inner self' which should choose: the individual should not be subject to pressure by external compulsive factors. But, as we saw in our discussion on freedom, the limits of his 'inner self' are logically arbitrary: it is we who choose the criteria according to which we say on one occasion that 'he' or 'a person' acted, and on another that the person was acted upon by some (external) factor, and our choice is suggested by sociological utility rather than dictated by logic or fact. The area of the self is not a fixture of reality; and the picture of a number of 'individuals', hard and impenetrable like billiard balls, who can somehow be entirely free (even from their own psychological make-up) provided we do not allow them to be knocked about by other individuals, is a false one. Thus, to go back to our original example, I may ask myself why I should prefer to let the schoolboy be made to act under pressure from the moral principles which his parents taught him in earlier years, rather than to force him myself to act in another way. I am answered, that those moral principles are now part of 'him', whereas my applied pressure is not part of him: so that in the first case he would be acting freely, which is a good thing, whereas in the second case I would be compelling him, which is a bad thing. But then, I say that there seems no logically compelling reason for regarding those moral principles as part of 'him': why should I not regard them as external to his 'inner self' or his 'true self', as I would regard kleptomania? That is, I refuse to be bullied by the commonly accepted decision about what counts as part of 'him', since such a decision is not incontestable: and I refuse to be bullied by commonly accepted usage, whereby no doubt it is true that one factor counts as compulsive and the other does not.

But of course there are good reasons for accepting wide criteria for the 'self', and not the narrow ones which I would be using in this example. If I do not use human beings as ends in themselves, in a wide sense of 'themselves', there is trouble. What sort of trouble? Well, it makes them unhappy, produces that sort of stagnation which arises from the lack of the conflict or interchange of different ideas and beliefs, results in that political tyranny which tends to corrupt the power-politician or the brain-washer, endangers the important overall belief that our values and motives may be wrong—and so on and so forth, as we read in the writings of liberal theorists of the western world. But this gives us a positive conception of freedom which, so far from being opposed to the men-as-machines thesis, actually stands in great need of it. For evidently we believe very strongly in expanding, widening and strengthening the human personality, not merely in protecting it. We object to certain types of influence, one might say, not so much because they are 'compulsive'—for to call them so implies a pre-decided picture of the self which is logically arbitrary—but because they are *restrictive*. And unless, using the men-as-machines outlook, we know something about the various factors and features which compose the human self, we shall hardly know what restricts it and what does not.

There are, indeed, two ways in which we can deal with our fellow men: ways which it is not sufficient to describe as 'using them as means' and 'using them as ends'. You can force them, bully them, bribe them, threaten them: and what is wrong with these methods is simply that you do not give people a chance to be themselves. Or you can give them facts, clarify things for them, offer them new experiences, explore the logical and psychological landscapes with them: and what is good about these methods is that you strengthen, clarify and enlarge the mind of the person you are dealing with. But there are plenty of cases where one is not sure whether one is doing one thing or the other. I allow a boy to act in such-and-such a way because he is very fond of me: is this a proper, healthy admiration which forms part of his true personality, or is it fanatical hero-worship which is restricting and warping that personality? I appeal to a boy's conscience: is this using, or helping to build up, his humanity, or is it a kind of moral bribery?

We may all agree, as defenders of freedom, that we want a strong, broad personality: and this agreement no doubt counts for a good deal, when we are faced by horribly real alternatives in the form of concentration camps and brain-washing. But it emphasises the importance of a clear understanding of human personality in scientific terms. It also emphasises that the Moralist's spiritual game, the game which reminds us to treat human beings holistically, must at all costs be guided by the Factualist's game of discovering what human beings are actually like, what makes them tick. For it is only too easy to use a pre-determined picture of what a human being is: to pre-empt one's criteria for the 'self', or the 'true self'. Thus, if you think that a human being is a child of the Christian God, you may also think that it is part of his true personality that he should feel guilty and sinful: and one could then set out to strengthen and clarify this part of him, maintaining (quite consistently) that this was not indoctrination at all, but would indeed minister to the positive end of freedom. Of course such a claim may be true: but it must be shown to be true to the satisfaction of all reasonable people.

Nobody wants rubber truncheons or brain-washing (except possibly in a very remote and depth-psychology sense of 'want'): but what people want will hardly defend us against more subtle abuses of freedom, more cunning restrictions on the human personality. (Indeed, in Huxley's *Brave New World* everyone, or almost everyone, wanted what they got: but we still do not like it, because their personalities were in fact restricted.) People can perfectly well want to be devoted servants of a Nazi or Soviet State, or want to feel guilty and sinful: that is, there are features of this kind in their personalities on which one can play. One might even say of the Nazi movement, for instance, that it showed that people needed at least some degree of communal faith and ideals, cashed out in ways which easily satisfied their aggressive instincts: or of religion, that human beings are in fact interlocked with the supernatural and could have experience of the divine. But if we act on these vague beliefs as if we had proved them, the chances are that we shall in fact restrict the personality instead of strengthening it: for we do not know the extent and nature of human needs of this kind. It is all-important, therefore, that we should spend a lot of time regarding human beings analytically, and show a due deference to whatever features of their personalities we actually find to be there. The holistic Moralist view is not worth much unless it is filled out by the facts.

What about the first Moralist game, the sociological game of reinforcing morality, educating, persuading, and so forth? This is subject to precisely those considerations which we have mentioned above. It too has to face the question of how far it fits the facts of human personality. Obviously it often fits them quite well. Children have to be educated, law and order has to be kept, people sometimes have to be made to feel disloyal or immoral, and so forth. But again, there is a temptation to suppose the game must be useful because no other game seems to do the same job. Can you educate children without using the moral pressure of Moralism? Perhaps you can. Would there be more crime and less hard work if we abolished retributive justice? Perhaps there wouldn't. Do you get the best out of people by making them feel disloyal and immoral when they go against Moralist concepts? Perhaps you don't. All this is to ask, perhaps, to what extent a man needs (or has to have) a super-ego, and what sort of super-ego suits him best; and at least one of our criteria for judging this would be whether this or that super-ego restricted or expanded his whole personality. Of course there would be others: we want law and order, hard work, etc. But above all, I take it, we all want a fuller and richer life: indeed perhaps we only want law and order and so forth in order to get a fuller and richer life. So that here too the positive conception of freedom is vital for the Moralist's moral-concept game.

Two points emerge in this assessment, which are worth making here not so much because we need to branch out into psychology as because the nature of the assessment needs illustration. First, psychological research discountenances the view that the human personality requires no framework of discipline and external pressure for a proper development. As one might expect, moral concepts have very deep psychological roots: and it is not so much the wicked, indoctrinating moralisers and schoolmasters who give us those nasty ideas about retributive justice, as basic and virtually inevitable factors which surround every human being in its very early years. We can be carried away by a right-wing desire to moralise at people, and thereby place unnecessary restrictions on them: but we can also be carried away by a radical desire to allow the personality to expand without applying even those restrictions which prevent it from disintegrating. Both are cases of failure to look at the facts.

Secondly, even after we have looked at the facts, we may still disagree. There may, for instance, be a genuine conflict between our desire to have unrestricted personalities and our desire to have integrated ones. Shall we produce people who are critical and aware, the content of whose conscious minds is very wide, who are flexible and sensitive? But then they may not be able to achieve contentment, to stand up to the battering of the outside world and the factors in their own unconscious minds. Or shall we produce more restricted people, sensible, uncritical, sound, *solid* personalities, who are contented and happy? But then, they will not be properly self-conscious and conscious of the outside world: isn't this like producing contented cows? And so on. So we may have to compromise; and on the compromise will depend the extent to which we are going to use the moral-concept game. Anyway, what are we going to count as a human personality? Just the conscious personality, the conscious desires, equilibrium and contentment? But this seems too restrictive: oughtn't we to include the unconscious as well? And what do we do about people who can be consciously happy, but only at the cost of having psychosomatic illnesses? Do we take the broad, optimistic, go-ahead view, and demand awareness and progress at all costs? Or shall we be sensible, draw in our psychological horns, and avoid suffering?

The assessment of such questions shows the Moralist's moral-concept game to be essentially a *brake*, a conservative force. We only want to apply the brake when it is necessary, when danger threatens: otherwise, perhaps, it is pleasant to go fast. Awareness of this point would, I think, produce a considerable change in the attitude of those who play the game. A schoolmaster, indeed, might say to himself: 'H'm, well, I think a moral lecture will meet the case for this boy', or 'Yes, a threat of expulsion might do the trick here', or 'We'll fix this chap by talking about justice'. But the ordinary person simply reacts to his fellows. In so far as he thereby plays the spiritual, holistic Moralist game, or at least implies it, we have no quarrel with him.

But playing the moral-concept game may or may not pay: and he ought to think about whether it will in fact pay or not. The Moralist may, of course, think that the moral-concept game is a good game to play in itself— he may play it neither because it pays nor because it reminds us of the importance of the spiritual game. But then we can indeed convict him of irrationality: there then seems no sensible purpose served by the game.

The moral life of the average man is generally guided by Moralist principles, uncritically adopted and deployed without sophistication. No doubt this is a pity: but philosophers have not always done all they could to remedy the situation in an appropriate way, chiefly because they have failed to realise the importance and variety of the uses of Moralism. Either they have tried, like Kant, to reinforce its concepts with an unconvincing metaphysic: or they have laboured, like the utilitarians, to prove that such concepts are a primitive and clumsy attempt at a Factualist ethic. Thus we seem forced to choose between some kind of absolute Moral Law, the metaphysical and logical basis of which modern philosophy has shown to be, at the very least, highly questionable: or a purely utilitarian morality, which would mean the total abandonment of a great many concepts and ways of thinking that we instinctively feel to be important.

Recent analytic philosophy has not been very helpful for this particular problem; for on the whole it has tended to the destruction of Moralism, or at least to the discredit of its logic. Thus, an analytic approach to such concepts as 'natural rights', 'the soul', 'free will', and so forth has resulted in a general impression that they consist mostly of metaphysical mists which the cool breath of the modern epistemologist has now dispelled. No doubt many errors have been usefully uncovered: but it is impossible to do justice to the use of such concepts by a purely logical or epistemological analysis, because they are far too closely related to social contexts. The same is also true of the specifically moral concepts of Moralism—'justice', 'honesty', 'truthfulness' and so on—which have, in fact, received comparatively little attention from modern philosophers. In neither aspect of its functions has Moralism been fairly treated.

We have already outlined these basic functions, the sociological and the spiritual.[1] We have seen that the first function is normally served by moral concepts ('justice', 'honesty', etc.) and the second by what one might call pseudo-metaphysical concepts ('the soul', 'free will', etc.). It will be hard to reach a full understanding of the importance of either unless we first realise that—to put it crudely—the *logic* of the concepts is not to be taken too seriously, even though their use and usefulness are matters of the greatest significance. There is, after all, not much to be said about the *logic* of rapping a child over the knuckles: yet this is similar to saying 'That's stealing!', and both have sociological importance. Similarly it would be absurd to study the logic of a demonstration protesting against atomic bombs or biological experiments unless we first understood its social purpose: which is, perhaps, similar to the social purpose served when people talk about 'human dignity' or 'natural rights'. Neither set of concepts is used only, or even chiefly, in contexts of discussion or ratiocination: both are used, as the concepts of morality must always be used, in a society where actions and decisions have to be taken all the time, and where a large proportion of our moral efforts

[1] See pp. 107–18.

will inevitably be devoted to averting disaster and preserving the established order.

Granted this, the importance of both functions of Moralism is plain enough. We need the continual reminders of standard moral concepts ('justice', 'honesty', etc.) to prevent society from degenerating into a chaos desired by nobody, and to prevent ourselves as individuals from falling into a moral disintegration which we at least unconsciously fear. The continual nudge of authority is essential both for social order and for individual sanity. We also need, particularly when vast changes threaten our security, the pseudo-metaphysical concepts of Moralism to remind us that men are human beings as well as machines, and that we can only undertake our Factualist calculations and changes as the servants, not the masters, of humanity. Talk of 'justice', 'honesty' and 'loyalty' defends us against chaos and insecurity: talk of 'human rights', 'the equality of men' and 'the soul' defends us against a wrongful exploitation.

Yet we need not think of the value of Moralism as purely negative. Though its concepts act as a brake and a defence, we may still admire and value the speed which the brake enables us to enjoy in security. Compared with the insecure existence of savages, or the tragic life of the individual under the most ruthless forms of totalitarian oppression, the stronghold which Moralism has built, and which it still protects, is no mean achievement. It would be logically vacuous to attempt any kind of assessment of the relative importance of Moralism and Factualism: each, in a quite different way, is plainly essential.

To conclude with a brief analogy: If you buy a new motor-car, you might be given—either on paper or verbally—three quite different kinds of instructions. First, there might be a book describing the workings of the car, together with plans, charts, blue-prints, and so on: this would give you all the facts about the car, much as Factualist researches hope to give us as many facts as possible about human nature. Secondly, there might be some specific instructions, such as 'Don't allow the water temperature to rise above 90 degrees', 'Always check the air pressure in the tyres', together with some rules of good driving, as in the Highway Code: these would act as perennial reminders, like the moral concepts of Moralism, to ensure safe driving and a sound car. Thirdly, there might be general reminders, such as 'Please remember that your car must be treated carefully at all times', or 'You are in control of a ton of potentially lethal metal: remember that the lives and safety of your neighbours are in your hands'. These act like the pseudo-metaphysical reminders of Moralism, telling you to value the car as a whole, and to treat with respect your dealings with other vehicles. All these three sets of instructions are important. We need the facts about the car, to keep it in working order, repair it when necessary, and perhaps improve its performance. We need the day-to-day reminders about maintenance and safe driving, to preserve the car properly and to avoid accidents. We need an overall attitude of respect towards the car and other cars, without which the other instructions will be neglected or abused. Each has its part to play: confusion only arises when one set of instructions is mistaken for another, or totally disregarded.

CHAPTER III

A METHOD FOR MORALS

THIS discussion of Moralist and Factualist games is not designed to make the players feel comfortable: though it is an essential preliminary to any further talk, because it is supposed to make them more aware of what the games are. We can now try to tie up this awareness with the more general doubts and hopes which we entertained in chapter I. Vague, anxiety-laden questions like 'How can I be certain that my morality is right?', 'How am I supposed to solve my moral problems?', or 'How can I tell right from wrong?', should now be easier to tackle. We can start in on methodology, on how to do ethics. We can make recommendations.

The first thing to notice is that these questions are all asked by people who are in doubt (otherwise they would not be genuine questions); people who have problems. They may be first-order moral problems ('Should I steal when I'm starving?'), or second-order ethical problems ('How should I think about stealing?', 'Is justice essential?'). But it is an important fact that, most of the time, people are not in doubt and do not have problems. The majority of people simply *use* their morality—perhaps blithely, perhaps sternly, but without very much anxiety or mental cross-questioning. What does the philosopher do about these people?

He had already done quite a lot, by showing that there *ought* to be doubt (if not anxiety), that people ought to realise that their moral lives are more problematic than they normally suppose. He makes the point, not because (or at least not only because) philosophy has a vested interest in doubt and problems, but because we now know that there is no question of certainty, or truth, or knowledge about 'right answers' to moral problems in the same sense as there is certainty and truth and knowledge about right answers to questions of fact.[1] If we cannot be certain in this sense, then, can we be certain at all? Well, we hardly know yet: meanwhile, it is wise to entertain doubts both about individual moral issues and about our general method of tackling such issues. This is past history: though it is the philosopher's business to make it present practice, by putting the relevant points very clearly and patiently before the public.

But we can do a bit more than this. We can show that certain games do not fit the context of doubt, and that other games do. The Moralist games are not games of knowing, finding out, or solving problems. They are not calculating games. Of course they are none the worse for that; and the philosopher has to point out their merits. He can say of one game 'Bear in mind the importance of preserving law and order', and of another 'Remember the importance of the total human personality, of positive freedom'. This still leaves us with the cases of doubt, with the problems. But now we have cleared away a lot of brushwood. When people feel Moralist tugs, we know what to do with them. Thus Professor Britton writes about Mill's utilitarian conception of justice:[2] 'Surely I ought to repay a debt whether my not doing so would weaken the social structure *or not*...I still feel that my loyalty to such institutions (*sc.* those which serve human

---

[1] See pp. 19–24.
[2] Karl Britton, *John Stuart Mill* (Pelican edition, 1953), pp. 55–6 (his italics).

happiness) does not rest *only* on considerations of their utility.' We say: 'Yes, there may be other facts which are relevant—failing to repay a debt may have bad effects on one's character, disloyalty to institutions may make one a less integrated person, etc. But if, having considered *all* the relevant facts, you still just *feel* dissatisfied, then your feelings are not useful for the Factualist game, for solving moral problems: they may be useful for some other game, but not for this.'

But how much help is this? We can say that the proper game to play with moral problems is the calculating game: and we may thus abolish or nullify those problems which arise solely because people are trying to play different games on the same board. We can also roughly describe the calculating, moral problem game; we can tell people to look at the facts, to be unprejudiced, to discuss reasonably, and so on. But if we try to do more—and we have, after all, undertaken to give at least the outlines of a methodology— we must abandon the game metaphor, or at any rate we must make more than formal comments upon the rules of the game. Thus, we might describe the formal rules of contract bridge or poker, so that it was clear to everybody what *sort* of games they were: but it would also be possible to make comments of a quite different sort. We could discuss the respective merits of different scoring systems, which might add to or detract from the merits of the games as a whole without changing their rules: or we could talk about how to play the games well, about what makes a good bridge player or a good poker player.

Once we are clear about the different types of games that can be played with moral language (and of course there is very much more to be said about this than I have begun to say), the game metaphor is not very helpful.

For we know how to play the Factualist, calculating game: we each have our moral criteria (our ends, standards, principles, values, or whatever), and we know we are to look at the facts with these criteria in mind. We know the formal rules, in other words. But there are other senses in which, perhaps, we do not altogether know how to play the game: that is, we do not know the best scoring system, or how to play the game successfully. At this point the philosopher may well hesitate: for these questions break into new territory, and it is not certain that they are specifically philosophical questions. But unfortunately it is just this territory which separates academic philosophy from the demands of the ordinary person—a territory which lies between the formal study of moral language and language-situations on the one side, and practical morality on the other. For these and other reasons, the philosopher may legitimately try to include at least some of this territory within his own domain; indeed, I believe it to be in some degree his duty to do so.

There are two obvious routes by which he may move into this territory. Having clarified the formal rules of the Factualist, calculating game, he may first ask the question: 'How good a game is this?' or 'What results can the game be expected to achieve?' This corresponds to the ordinary person's concern about certainty and agreement in morality: he wants to know how far the game will carry us towards such certainty and agreement. Since the playing of the game depends formally upon the acceptance of ultimate criteria, we can ask how and why we come to accept ultimate criteria in other fields besides the field of morality, or what sort of agreement is possible in our acceptance of ultimate ethical criteria, or what are the chances of such agreement. We can study the game, not formally and analytically, but informally and as a whole. In the second place, the philosopher may ask the question 'How can the game best be played?' or 'What makes a good player?' This also corresponds to the ordinary person's concern about certainty and agreement, but in a different way: he is not now worried about whether the game itself can be expected to produce satisfactory results, but about learning to play it properly. Here the philosopher can usefully comment on the best attitude which the ordinary man can take to the game—the most appropriate stance with which to face it, so to speak. I shall try to say something about each of these points in turn.

I. CRITERIA AND AGREEMENT

Let us first consider how it is that we come to accept criteria in other fields. The respective statements "That is a good knife', 'This is a red book', 'The earth goes round the sun' and 'Twice two are four' have quite properly been placed by philosophers in different logical classes. Such statements may differ in meaning and in the type of information they give, in point of syntax, verifiability and a host of other ways. But it is a common feature of all of them that they are easily verifiable, albeit by widely differing methods. Nobody nowadays would have any difficulty in finding out, or at any rate in knowing how to find out, whether they were true or not. Of course, this is simply because the verification and criteria appropriate to each are almost universally agreed among present-day men. We might describe these statements as naturalistic, because their truth or falsehood can be determined by sole reference to natural phenomena. But it is important to note that by saying that their truth can be determined thus, we would naturally mean that almost *everyone* today can in fact determine it. In other words, there is general agreement about how it is to be determined.

It is important to note this, because it sheds light on the question of the general acceptance of criteria. This acceptance has an effect on language, in that the criteria, once firmly established, exercise a predominating influence on the meaning of the statements with which they are connected. Thus, as we have seen, it would be nonsense to say 'This is a good knife, but it does not cut well, breaks easily, etc.', or 'This is a red book, but its colour has a wavelength which we normally assign to blue, and it contains no print or writing, is intangible, weighs nothing, etc.' Naturally nobody would ever wish to say this, for the simple reason that the criteria of verification have been tailored to fit the knives and the red books that we already have experience of: it is only in borderline cases that we come to think about what these criteria actually consist of, and only in such cases that we may wish to change them. But at present, in the vast majority of the statements we make, the criteria, as it were, logically determine the meaning or an essential part of the meaning.

On the level of ordinary language, therefore, it is absurd to challenge those statements which we already know to be true by virtue of firmly established criteria. But on a more sophisticated level, the challenge is legitimate: and it is to be interpreted on this level, not as a request for certainty or justification in the normal sense, but rather as a basic attack on our normal usage. For example, a man might ask 'How do I know the sun will rise tomorrow?' We can explain to him that he cannot expect logical certainty, because he is demanding knowledge about matters of fact: 'the sun will rise tomorrow' is not a logically necessary statement. We can explain further that he already has inductive knowledge that the sun will rise, and we can quote him the appropriate evidence for this knowledge. He can 'give good reasons', 'be certain', 'be justified' and 'know' that the sun will rise, in all the normal senses of those words. But the man may reiterate his question in another form. He cannot sensibly say 'How do I know that these reasons you quote are really good reasons?', for it is generally agreed what are to count as 'good reasons' for the sun's rising. But what he can say is 'Why should I be a party to this general agreement about what count as "good reasons"? Why should I accept your criteria for certainty and knowledge?'

Of course this is a very unusual thing to say. Normally people acquiesce in established criteria and established standards. People who are colour-blind admit that they are colour-blind: they do not usually say that they just prefer different criteria for colours. The word 'colour-blind' suggests that the vision of the majority of people is in some sense 'right', and the vision of a small minority defective. There is an accepted method of verifying colours, which ultimately depends on our ability to identify and distinguish objects by visual comparison. We can also carry out a cross-check on this by measuring the wavelengths of the light-rays reflected from the objects. Since this verification is established, a colour-blind person who accepts it is bound often to admit himself 'wrong' about colours. If everyone else says a colour is pink, he cannot say it is blue, provided that he accepts the standard criteria for colours.

But neither the man who is colour-blind, nor the man who feels doubts about the sun's rising, is logically compelled to accept these established criteria. If he accepts them, he is logically compelled to abide by them in his discourse: but that is a very different thing. No doubt if a man did not accept any of the standard criteria which are established, he would find it very difficult to communicate with his fellows: but if there is compulsion here, it is psychological and not logical compulsion. Nor, in point of fact, is it always psychologically necessary to accept even the most well-established criteria. Those people who still believe that the earth is flat have not done so. Of course, such people may be illogical about the matter: that is, they may hold views which are logically contradictory. But it is always open to them to deny the whole apparatus of verification by which their fellows assume the earth to be round.

What is accepted as fact, such as the sun's rising, the existence of tables, and all the thousands of things of which we speak every day, depends therefore (logically speaking) on what are the accepted criteria of verification. In only one case is the acceptance of these criteria logically necessary: and that is the case in which they can be logically justified in terms of higher criteria. But such logical justification is somewhat different. For example, imagine a man who is colour-blind and who wishes to choose the right colours for decorating his house: that is, the colours which will please his friends, who have normal vision. Granted this end, it can be shown to him that in order to achieve it, he will have to employ the standard criteria for colours. If he does not employ these criteria, but prefers his own, he will not achieve his end. Here the higher criteria, the criteria which determine what colour-verification to adopt, are simply 'whatever verification will best enable me to please my friends'; these justify the lower criteria, the actual criteria for determining colours. Similarly, if a man wishes to be able to communicate with his fellows and to be understood by them, it would be illogical of him to refuse to adopt the current criteria which they use: for if his criteria for the existence of tables, colours, temperature and everything else bear no relation to those in common use, he will not be able to communicate satisfactorily. But this is a quite ordinary sort of justification concerned with ends and means: it is not the linguistic form of logical compulsion which may be applied to a man who already accepts the current criteria for colours, temperatures, and so forth. To say 'I want to communicate, but I do not want to use the current criteria for the application of words in the language people speak' may be mistaken, but is not nonsense: but to say 'This is pink, although everyone with normal vision will always think it blue' is nonsense, in ordinary language at least.

Nevertheless, we do accept many of the current criteria because they satisfy our ends: although the process is largely unconscious because it usually occurs in early childhood, when we are as yet unacquainted with inductive logic. For example, children desire the satisfaction of their needs for food and security: they learn at an early stage that this satisfaction can be more easily achieved by the use of language in accordance with the rules. Thus, the criteria for the application of 'Mummy', 'sweets', 'oranges' and so forth are taken over by the child from current usage, represented by the usage of its parents. Granted the child's end, it is obviously logical for it to adopt these criteria, since by them it may satisfy its end. A great part of the activity of children, and of adults, may be described as putting their experience in order: building up out of their sense-data and their other experiences a formal pattern of the world which will enable them to live more pleasantly or happily. This depends largely on the acquisition of empirical knowledge, which in turn entails the acceptance of numerous criteria for empirical beliefs and statements.

There are, nevertheless, cases where the adoption of criteria appropriate to the satisfaction of ends is refused. This is often due to a conservatism or an unwillingness to make the necessary effort to learn the rules. Thus, a man born blind may be cured of his blindness at an advanced age, but be unwilling to make proper use of his new vision. When blind, he was able to verify the existence, properties and qualities of objects by his senses of touch and hearing: he had his own set of criteria which he used satisfactorily. On recovering his sight, he is faced with the possibility of learning a completely new set of criteria for objects: and often a great deal of pressure is required to make him learn. He has to work hard to discover what visual experiences correspond to what objects or attributes of objects. But the advantages of these criteria—for example, that one can use them to discover the attributes of objects which one cannot touch—can be pointed out to him: and if he wishes for these advantages, and considers them worth the effort of attaining, his only rational course is to learn the criteria.

It is in such test cases that we become conscious of our criteria and any reasons we may have for adopting them. One important example may be found in the natural sciences. It is by now generally accepted that one of the chief ends of scientific investigation is the ability to predict. In the field of microscopic physics, for instance, the clarification of this higher criterion is of extreme importance: many scientists now use the prediction-value of scientific statements as virtually the only test of their truth. For in this field, we are no longer dealing with visible and tangible objects having colours and shapes: indeed, it is questionable whether we are dealing with objects at all. The difficulty of determining whether electrons or ions are objects has suggested that, in such cases, scientists need not be interested in the question (though philosophers may be). What they are interested in is whether useful information can be given about matter in such terms: whether the theories requiring these concepts enable us better to predict the behaviour of matter, and hence to construct atomic piles, bombs, and so forth. We become conscious of our interests and ends in such cases, because they lie outside our normal experience of nature: in other cases, our ends are taken for granted.

It is possible, however, to deny not only current criteria but also commonly-accepted ends. Primitive peoples may prefer to believe in an unpredictable god of thunder and lightning rather than to accept the natural laws which would enable them to understand and predict their occurrence. Lunatics, refusing to accept the normal criteria for physical objects, may prefer to satisfy their own inexplicable ends and to regard themselves as poached eggs requiring a substratum of toast. There may be insane men who think that it is just as likely that unsupported bodies will suddenly rise upwards as that they will continue to fall downwards. But to call these people lunatic or insane means (*inter alia*) that they have rejected current criteria: it does not mean that there are logically compulsive arguments for accepting the criteria.

In the last analysis, therefore, the case with science and other empirical knowledge is the same as it is with ethics. Briefly, we cannot logically compel people to adopt any criterion, if they choose to deny every criterion. We might notice *en passant* that deductive knowledge is no better off: for in order logically to compel people to accept deductions, it is necessary that they first accept the so-called 'laws of thought', or the simple rules of logic. It is quite open to them to refuse to do so, and also to refuse to accept any higher ends which the rules of logic may help them to satisfy. But the striking fact about the comparison of ethics with other knowledge, and of ultimate ethical criteria with other sorts of criteria, is that the former are not accepted, whereas the latter are. Man wishes to make sense of the world, and to set his experience in some sort of coherent order. To put things in order, it is necessary to have some system of judging where to put them: in other words, to have criteria. These criteria need not be clearly or consciously conceived or expressed, but it is logically necessary that they should exist if there are to be judgements or any process of selection; for the word 'criterion' means simply 'a principle of judgement'. Much of our language is used in reference to these criteria, and hence, in the last analysis, to the process of selection which precedes them. Thus a primitive man comes to grasp a criterion of goodness and badness for foodstuffs, the criterion being based mainly on whether it is pleasant to eat them or not, or whether eating them produces unpleasant results (such as illness) in the long run. He calls rotten meat, deadly nightshade and unripe apples 'bad', fresh meat, corn and ripe apples 'good'. He does this because he has tried both classes of foodstuffs, and knows the results of eating both. If his friends do the same, and the results of their appreciation of the foodstuffs are similar, there arises a criterion of naturalistic goodness in respect of foodstuffs. Similarly, he may wish to draw a distinction between pieces of flint that are good for making flint knives, and pieces of flint that are bad: he may describe the first as 'hard', 'sharp', or 'easily chipped', and the second by the opposite terms. After his friends have had sufficient experience of pieces of flint and flint knives, they may come to adopt criteria of hardness, sharpness and the ability to be easily chipped. In this way numerous distinctions of practice or experience might be drawn, and (because communication is a valuable tool) these distinctions might be expressed in distinctions of language.

This comes about entirely because man is a purposive animal. He wants to distinguish between foodstuffs, pieces of flint, and innumerable other things, and to establish the distinctions. In doing so, he relies on the assumption that other men have ends which are similar to his own, or desires and aversions which are similar to his own: and this is often the case. Thus, he commends certain food-stuffs as being 'good', on the criterion that they give him pleasure, do not make him ill, and so forth; and because other men have the same ends, the word 'good' is accepted in this context. Similarly, other men have purposes which make the distinctions between hardness and softness, sharpness and bluntness, and the like, useful to them. This does not, of course, imply that usefulness is itself a criterion for our application of particular words in particular cases. The meaning of the words, and our justification of our use of them, is to be found by reference to their own criteria or the methods of verifying them. But the purpose of these criteria, in the last resort, is the satisfaction of the purposes of men: they are used as means to various ends. Of course, it would not be possible to give an account of all the words in our language in quite such narrow terms. We cannot in this way account for the appearance of words such as 'and', 'if', 'therefore' and similar words,

which have a strictly logical function: though even in
their case we may say that their logical function furthers
the end of human communication, which in turn enables
men to achieve their purposes. But it is fair to say that our
numerous nouns and adjectives, for example, exist because
we wish to symbolise objects or attributes which we have
differentiated: and our differentiation, and the establish-
ment of criteria for differentiation, can usually be best
understood by reference to human purposes.

A case might plausibly be made out for saying that the
nature of fundamental human knowledge has more in
common with ethics than with empirical knowledge. For
in accepting both moral and empirical criteria, the ultimate
question which might be posed is not 'Which are the *true*
criteria?' for it is plain that the acceptance of criteria is
a *choice*. The question is rather 'Which criteria *ought* we to
accept?' This is not the sort of question for which either
present-day ethics or empirical knowledge caters at all. It
is, I suppose, usually to be interpreted as a question about
appropriate means to an established end. Thus if we desire
predictability, we can meaningfully say that we 'ought' to
adopt certain criteria for the truth of various scientific
assertions: or if we want objects to be useful, we can say
that we 'ought' to adopt our present criteria for, for
example, the goodness of knives. But in any case we are
using a quite different kind of discourse, and on a quite
different level, from our normal discourse about 'ethics'
and 'empirical knowledge'. The distinction is useful at
a low level, but not at the level of ultimate criteria. And
at the level of ultimate criteria, just because they are ultimate, no logical distinction between the criteria themselves
is of any value. What is of value is a logical commentary on
the ways in which the criteria may come to be accepted.

It should now seem plausible that we may come to agree about our ultimate ethical criteria, as about our other criteria—provided we can overcome certain obstacles. The most important of these, from a purely academic point of view, is the difficulty of collecting enough relevant facts. The chief reason why facts, and the unprejudiced appreciation of facts, have been difficult to obtain in ethics is because we have not been able to obtain anything like experimental conditions. Suppose we were disputing whether sexual purity was good or not. We might be regarding chastity as an end, an ultimate criterion of goodness, or alternatively as a means to some such end as 'making oneself a good person'. It makes no difference which, because in order to have any chance of settling the dispute, we need both facts and an appreciation of them which are at present beyond our grasp. We need to discover what is the result of chastity upon a person and on his neighbours: what its results are upon individual characters and actions, and under what conditions these results obtain. Here we are learning facts: but plainly these facts are not forthcoming at present. In the second place, it would be useful to be able to compare two people who are equal in all other respects except chastity, to be free of prejudice about the matter, and to appreciate which of them we prefer: and this too is difficult, if not impossible. But without these facts and this appreciation it would be hard to reach unanimity about chastity.

Unfortunately we are quite often in this unfavourable position, particularly with regard to appreciation. For instance, it is possible for the same man to react to two different pictures, or two different pieces of music; but it is much more difficult for the same man to reach an appreciation of two differently organised countries, and (though he may appreciate the lives of others) it is impossible for him to live two different lives himself for purposes of comparison. Yet such appreciations might be necessary before we could reach unanimity about, say, the value of political freedom, or the value of a life of self-sacrifice. A large part of the trouble lies in the fact that what we have to appreciate is often on a very large scale. People's actions and character interact with those of other people: states of affairs produce other states of affairs: political systems, especially, require appreciation which must be macroscopic not only in place, but in time. We cannot be certain what we want until we can appreciate our ethical subject-matter against a more general background.

The evidence that agreement is possible, however, is more formidable than may be supposed. For it can be shown that in a great many ethical questions unanimity has been achieved, and by precisely those means which we have described. There are certain ethical criteria which are unanimously held: it would be agreed, for example, that stealing, war, murder, continual drunkenness, addiction to drugs, and so forth, are evil. On a more sophisticated level, we could reduce these specific evils to a smaller number: we could say that we disapproved of these things because we disapproved of social chaos, loss of life, pain, lack of self-control, and so on. We might even say that in what we considered to be an 'ideal society' these things would not exist. But although these criteria might be ultimate, they are nevertheless unanimous. Our moral judgements coincide to an enormous extent. I can see no other explanation for this than that we have had sufficient experience of these evils, and their opposites, to know what we 'really' want. Moral issues over which we are not unanimous, such as the value of chastity, self-sacrifice, and punishment, and complicated political questions about what sort of government or economy we ought to have, where we are equally in disagreement, are exactly those questions in which we lack due experience. We know what happens when people steal or make war: we do not know what happens when people are unchaste or are governed according to the principles of Plato's *Republic*. We have experience and appreciation of theft and war: we have not any direct and specific appreciation of chastity or a Platonic government. Thus, in the one case we have both knowledge of the facts, and opportunity for appreciation: in the other we have neither.

Psychology, as well as the collective and disorganised experience of all men, has already influenced our ethics in the direction of unanimity. Fewer people today in our society believe firmly in the value of retributive punishment; and this is at least partly due to the demonstration on the part of psychologists of what actually happens to people who are treated, or punished, in certain ways. Certain dogmas concerned with 'conscience' and 'willpower' have come to be abandoned as a result of the progress of psychological knowledge. Ultimate and unshakable beliefs on the part of educationalists about how children should be brought up, what subjects they should be made to learn, and so forth, have been gradually relinquished. These are empirical facts, and facts illustrative of moral questions which we should all admit to be of the highest importance. Even more significant is the point that, under the influence of psychology, new ways of expressing ultimate criteria are coming to be adopted. Stock criteria such as 'happiness', which is as old as human history, and 'evolutionally valuable', which is at least as

old as Darwin, 'sanity,' 'harmony', 'a balanced personality', are less depended upon than they were; and our
vices are no longer describable merely by their old names,
but by words such as 'obsession','megalomania','complex',
'fixation' and so forth. And although we are not logically
compelled to believe that a certain trait of character is
bad just because a psychologist calls it a fixation, it is
noticeable that the study of psychology nevertheless tends
to result in increased human agreement about the un-
desirability of such traits.

It seems, then, that the evidence for the likelihood of
eventual unanimity is overwhelming: and what is especially
significant, it all points the same way. We have not yet
met a case where we have had proper experience and yet
failed to agree. We can, therefore, only believe that proper
experience will probably lead to unanimity in the acceptance of ultimate ethical criteria, just as it has led to
unanimity in other cases. This belief is not logically
necessary. It is possible, for example, that knowledge of
the facts may be denied us, owing to the break-down of
psychology or the refusal of human beings to discover the
facts. There may be an atomic war which lands us back in
the dark ages: people may go mad: we may put an end to
human life. All these are possibilities. Nobody is laying
any bets about the progress of ethics. But at least we have
the possibility of a methodology.

The classical philosophers were correct in supposing
that it was necessary to describe 'the true end of man' if
the right means of achieving that end were to be discovered and proved. Their mistake was to suppose that
either the end or the means could be discovered without due
experience: and this means, in the case of ethics, as in that
of physical health, knowledge of enough facts to see what

men are actually like: how they behave, what are the causes of that behaviour, what different types of behaviour result in, and so forth. Once enough people come to have sufficient experience of health, either in themselves or in others, there is no question in their minds but that this state is their ultimate end. But without the knowledge of what behaviour produces what effects, it will be impossible for them to decide what is 'health' and what is not. A tribe whose staple diet consists partly of semi-poisonous berries and fermented grapes may come to regard stomach-aches and drunkenness as part of 'the natural end of man', simply because they have no idea of the causes of these ailments. Knowledge of facts is necessary, in such cases, for the ability to decide rationally.

The parallel between health and morals is of course only an analogy, and not a proof. But it illustrates an essential point made by many classical philosophers which, though now generally neglected, is nevertheless valid. The point is that, though it is not logically compulsory to derive ultimate ethical criteria from knowledge of empirical facts, it is generally the case that we do actually come to do so. By learning more about the human body and how it works, we come both to accept an ideal state of 'health', and a set of rules for achieving that state. Of course it is logically open to anyone to say that he does not prefer health, but would rather be unhealthy. He could even say that it is better to be unhealthy; this would mean that he did not accept the generally established criteria for health. But hardly anyone does in fact say this, because most people have had sufficient experience to judge what they want, and what rules they are going to adopt to get what they want. It may appear remarkable that an overwhelming majority of people should want the same thing (and consequently adopt the same rules), but it is the case. As with aesthetics, the more we know and the more chances we have to appreciate, the more we tend to agree, and the more unanimous we become in respect of our ultimate criteria. By talking of the 'true nature of man', the classical philosophers intended to suggest that man's mental and spiritual life, including the sphere which we now call 'morals', could be dealt with in the same way.

According to the classical parallel, the minds and spirits of men, and the states of affairs in societies and communities which come under ethical surveillance, can be dealt with as we have dealt with health; or, in the last resort, as we would deal with (for example) a machine or a motor-car. Imagine that we are presented with what is in fact a motor-car, but do not know how we ought to use it, since we know nothing of its purpose or the ways of operating it. We might, in our ignorance, use its roof for sunbathing, its fenders for shaving-mirrors, and its engine (if we could start it) simply for making a loud noise. We could also have great fun with its headlights and its horn. Sects might arise, stating dogmatically that the 'true' use of this uncomprehended object was so-and-so, or such-and-such; that the all-important part of it was this, that, or the other; that people ought not to sunbathe on the roof, or sound the horn without first offering up a prayer, on the grounds that this violated its 'true nature'; and perhaps eventually different people would simply accept different criteria of behaviour in regard to the motor-car, and agree to differ in a spirit of mutual tolerance. But, after many years of patient striving, sufficient might be known about it to understand how it really ought to be used: that it could, if supplied with petrol and properly maintained, perform tasks and functions which we should all consider desirable. We would also know what its 'proper state' should be: the plugs should be clean, the tyres inflated, the engine free from rust, and so on. We would come to have a conception of the 'ideal motor-car', and the rules for making motor-cars ideal.

It would, I must repeat, still be possible for recalcitrant people to say that the motor-car should be used for quite different purposes, however many facts about its operation had been discovered: but it is intrinsically improbable that there would be very many such people. One way of treating and using the motor-car would come to be accepted as the right way. Having achieved the desired unanimity, we could then be certain of all our value-judgements, imperatives and so on in respect of the motor-car. We would not cease to pay attention to those who still refused to accept our ultimate criteria, for it would always be possible to improve on them by the invention or discovery of new and better ways of treating the motor-car, ways discovered by the learning of more facts and the appreciation of more situations. Inventors of such improvements would persuade us to change our ultimate criteria in favour of others.

Naturally we can think of objections to this methodology. Why shouldn't one set of criteria suit one person, and another set suit another—even if we know all the facts? Or why shouldn't we change our criteria in the course of time? Indeed, isn't the whole point of value-words like 'good', speaking sociologically, that they leave it open to us to do so—that nobody can tie them down permanently to descriptive criteria? Plainly we *need* these words: won't this method in the end (if it is successful, which one doubts) do away with the possibility of variety and change in our criteria? But this is quite acceptable, we answer. The method is only intended to bring our different moral judgements into line with each other, on the facts which we actually possess; not to produce permanent uniformity, a sort of strangulation of ethics. We may well think that one sort of life is good for one man, and another for another (just as one machine works best in this way, and another machine in that). Similarly, criteria may change in the course of time: indeed, they obviously will. To call a man 'good' in A.D. 2000 will be to grade him highly because he has certain qualities: but by A.D. 3000 we may be able to produce men with hitherto unheard-of qualities. Then, perhaps, we will call these men 'good' and the A.D. 2000 man 'not so good'—or even 'bad'. This is not worrying. 'Good' grades and influences choice, and one cannot choose or grade what is not available. Nobody would have been wrong in saying there was 'good drama' and 'good music' in A.D. 1000, just because Shakespeare and Beethoven are better than most drama and music in A.D. 1000, or refuse to call Shakespeare and Beethoven 'good' just because super-Shakespeares and super-Beethovens might appear in the future.

Or again, we may wonder whether this methodology is not naïve: whether it does not miss the whole point of morality, which is surely to settle conflicts between one person or group of people and another. Perhaps the facts might show such conflicts to be irreconcilable? But we have not pretended to produce a methodology which leads to Utopia. The facts are there, and we must face them and do the best we can with them: for if we do not face them, they will surely get their revenge. It would admittedly be naïve, or at least optimistic, to pretend that the facts of reality have been presented to us like a box of bricks, all of which fit together perfectly once we see what sort of building to make.

There may indeed be conflicts, but I believe there are also grounds for optimism. First, it may be true that conflicts of ends only occur when one party to the conflict is not actually pursuing the end which is most satisfactory to him. This is to say that those ends which are in fact most satisfactory to all human beings, though they may be different, do not conflict, or need not do so if our communal life is well organised socially and politically. Thus, supposing one man is a sadist, and his pursuit of the end which seems most satisfactory to him consists largely of inflicting pain on others; and suppose further that the end of other people involves a painless life. Then it might be empirically true that the sadist is not actually pursuing the truly satisfactory end: that we should be able to persuade him by an empirical demonstration that he could find some different end (which did not involve the infliction of pain upon others) just as satisfactory, or more satisfactory. Secondly, we might be able to point to some end which was universally satisfactory to everyone, and such that it could not logically involve conflict. For instance, if the behaviour-pattern of Christian charity (interpreted in the sense of furthering the ends of others, and not pursuing your own ends when they interfere with those of others) were capable of being proved the most satisfactory end for all men, then we should have no logical problem: merely the practical problem of persuading men to accept the view that it was the most satisfactory end. And since this view would be based on empirical or psychological fact, our persuasion would be rational.

The fact that, when two ends conflict, we still believe that one person is 'right' and the other 'wrong', despite all the subjectivism of modern moral philosophy, seems to me to show that we still believe in some possibility of settling the issue. I do not think that this is merely an irrational hope, or the result of an irrational belief in 'absolute' or 'objective' values. It is, I think, the belief that if enough psychological facts were known, and provided that our consideration of them were unprejudiced, we should not need to have conflicting views. Hence the perennial temptation to say that the sadist, for instance, cannot 'really want' to pursue the end which involves sadism. If you verify what he wants by seeing what he actually pursues, it is obviously untrue. But if to say this means that no man's most satisfactory end involves sadism, then it may very well be true. The psychologists' concept of a 'healthy' or 'sane' mind may be given a purely descriptive meaning: that is the sort of mind which is found by men to be most satisfactory. And it seems to me more probable than improbable that all sane men will have minds which possess basically similar features, and that they will pursue ends which may be different, but will not conflict. After all, we are all human beings; and though we are different, we are not impossibly different. That is why 'inhuman' has a descriptive as well as an evaluative meaning.

But in any case, it has not proved beyond our powers to devise a mechanism for resolving such conflicts, if they exist. This is the mechanism of morality, law or convention and its purpose is simply to allow those who live together in a community to live the most satisfactory lives possible, consonant with the fact that they are living in a community. Hence nearly all peoples adhere to the principle of not stealing, because it is in their interest to do so. It is in their interest, not necessarily because they would be caught and punished if they stole, but because the preservation and safety of his property is a necessary part of each man's most satisfactory end. In theory, so to speak, it might be true that each man's most satisfactory end consisted in stealing but not being stolen from; but in pointing out to each man what his most satisfactory end is, we are considering what it is in practice, not what it might be if things were different. It will usually be irrational of me to steal, because this will in practice involve my being stolen from: and the net result is not the most satisfactory life possible for me.

It is not necessary to claim that there are no conflicts of satisfactory ends, or that all such conflicts are resolvable by an appeal to enlightened self-interest. Speaking as philosophers, we could say simply that only the criterion of what end a man will find satisfactory can provide reasons for pursuing this end or that one, and that if these ends do conflict, men must work out the problem for themselves with the aid of persuasion, agreement, compromise, or violence. If two ends really do conflict, despite all that self-interest can do, then no doubt the victory will go to the stronger or the more subtle. But I think it likely that Plato's famous picture of the tyrant in the *Republic* is psychologically accurate, and that consequently the logic of his argument ('Do not be a tyrant, because it is not satisfactory') is sound; moreover I should suspect that this applies to some extent to anyone whose chosen end involves thwarting the satisfactory ends of other men. The essential interdependence of men, and the fact that it is either not possible or in the alternative not satisfactory to act as an outlaw, seems to me to lend considerable support to this view.

2. RATIONAL MORALITY

We have spent some time making the point that men wish to fulfil themselves, and that morality serves human purposes. This is an encouraging point, in so far as we now know not only what game we are supposed to be playing, but also that the game can carry us a very long way—perhaps sufficiently far to give us that certainty and agreement for which we originally hoped. But it might seem discouraging in so far as we now know that there is no simple answer to all our moral problems; that we shall not get our morality straight until we get our purposes straight. The danger of laying down ultimate criteria lies in the implication that our purposes are straight already. Certainly, there are simple methods of detecting when we have made an unwise choice: we may feel regret, or be aware of conflict and frustration: we may have an inkling that we have missed something, that we have not risen to heights which we could have climbed. But these conscious methods are too superficial to be of much use. The human race has been quietly pursuing happiness (called by different names) for some thousands of years: in so far as we have gained in the pursuit, our gain has come more from the greater understanding of our own purposes, and the means of fulfilling them, than from worrying about morality. For not all our purposes are clear to us: many of our drives are unconscious: a good deal of the human machine is not exposed to view.

The fact that it is *we* who are choosing what is most satisfactory for *us* makes it more difficult. Different purposes come to seem more important to us at different times: different parts of the machine make themselves felt on various occasions. The temptation is therefore always to repress or disown certain features of our personalities which seem to us to get in the way. We disown the pleasures of attachment and of the senses, and take to Stoicism: or we disown the need for courage and self-sufficiency and become Epicureans. We may be peculiarly sensitive to the demands of conscience, and turn to Kant: or peculiarly insensitive to them, and turn to Bentham. In an extreme case we may even try to abolish rather than solve the problem of reconciling our different purposes, simply by trying to remove completely one of the features of the case, or to disclaim all responsibility for fitting it into a satisfactory pattern. Thus we might say (almost *sans phrase*, as some early Christian authorities did) 'sex is bad': or we could bring up children in a way designed to quash any instincts of competition or aggression with which they might unfortunately happen to have been born, as certain progressive educators have tried to do. But this is obviously cheating. We want to use all the bricks in the box, not to leave the more difficult ones out of our building: for they may also be the more exciting ones, if we can only learn how to fit them in. Moreover, the features we try to disown have a way of making themselves felt despite all that we can do. The underground mechanisms still go on working, even though we pretend that they are not there.

Generally the turn of the roundabout, both at academic and at practical levels, is a sign of healthy conflict. The philosophical dialectic of Stoicism and Epicureanism, Kant and the utilitarians, and so forth, at least has the advantage of drawing attention to the wide variety of mechanisms for which we must cater; and if the mores of a society change from puritanism to hedonism, back to puritanism again and then back to more hedonism, we may perhaps expect to gain a little more genuine understanding each time the roundabout turns. But we shall not gain very much until we realise that it is a roundabout and that it only turns because we do not seem to have the patience or the courage to stop it, and walk quietly and observantly round it in order to gain a balanced view of all the dazzling shapes that now bewilder us with their rapid succession.

Thus although we may hope that eventual agreement in ethics is in principle possible, we must also realise that it is not just the absence of factual knowledge which prevents us from realising that hope. Our own unwillingness to face the facts in a proper way—our refusal to adopt the right approach—is a still more important cause. It is so common an experience in our lives that the moral philosopher must do justice to it if he is not to seem hopelessly academic, and hence to fail to meet the ordinary man's demands. There is the case where we know quite well what we ought to do, but will not or cannot do it: where our will-power is inadequate. Thus, a man might know that he ought to go to the dentist, but simply be unable to bring himself to do it. Or a consideration of the facts might point to one course of action, but we become distracted by other considerations: thus, it might seem generally beneficial to let a guilty person go unpunished, but we decide to punish him in the interests of justice. Both these situations may arise even when all the facts are known. Further, there are many cases where the relevant facts are not known but where we refuse to adopt an appropriately agnostic attitude to the moral issues involved. Thus, most people have strong views about sexual morality, even though they are not possessed of the facts. Most modern philosophers tend to regard such cases as outside their province, since they appear due to emotional rather than intellectual inadequacy. But it is very much the philosopher's business to give as clear an outline as possible of a rational approach to morality, even if people have to turn to the priest or the psychiatrist for assistance in adopting such an approach. To put it another way: it is possible to describe the cases of irrationality mentioned above in conceptual terms as well as in psychological ones. No doubt it is psychological weakness which has caused the conceptual breakdown: but the conceptual breakdown is there just the same, and can be described.

As we said earlier,[1] this can best be regarded as a question of adopting the right *stance* in the face of morality; and our advice here will be like the advice of the tennis-coach who tells his pupils to put themselves in this or that position, to avoid the temptation to do so-and-so, to practise doing such-and-such, and so forth. From this point of view practical morality appears as a kind of skill which can be acquired by practice and instruction. Unlike other advisers, however, the philosopher will not tell his pupils how to practise this or that way of living, or how to live up to any particular moral problems, in what frame of mind to take moral decisions, what attitude to adopt towards morality in general, and so on. He does not know, and does not pretend to know, what decisions should ideally be made in each case, any more than the tennis-coach pretends to know exactly what shots his pupil should make in the next match. Nor does he have to be a first-rate performer in practical morality himself, any more than the tennis-coach has to be a first-rate performer in tennis tournaments. The special skill of each depends solely on their expert understanding of the game which they teach.

[1] See pp. 30–2.

By far the most important point to be made is the simple one that the appropriate attitude to morality is a *rational* attitude. This is a point which almost everyone would accept in the present context—that is, in a context where we are discussing morality in a philosophical or academic way—but which hardly anybody accepts in other contexts, or really takes to heart. As we have noticed,[1] most people do not really *think* about their moral problems at all: they just *feel* about them. Plainly there is nothing irrational in having feelings: what is irrational is that such people take their feelings as self-guaranteeing, that they treat them as carrying their own justification with them. Most people adopt a course of action either after a sharp mental conflict, or by a kind of vague mental drifting in one direction or another. They fail to realise that feelings are not, in themselves, evidence: they may be used as evidence, as the raw material for taking decisions, but should not themselves be allowed to decide anything. We are too content to allow our minds to become a battle-ground in which our feelings merely conflict—sometimes with the energy of wild beasts released from their cages, sometimes with the weariness and frustration of a long-drawn battle.

This point would be hardly worth making, were it not that many people intellectually acquiesce in the situation. It is not simply that they cannot help themselves: it is rather that they do not want to, because they do not really think that they ought to. Though an irrational attitude to empirical problems, such as questions of science or medicine, would be regarded as at best childish and at worst insane, the same attitude to moral problems is considered quite acceptable. We are content to allow our reason to be the slave of our passions, and not satisfied to allow it to be

[1] See p. 30.

merely their servant and adjudicator: we prefer to allow our feelings to choose for us, and even take a certain pride in resigning our own choice to them. Often we say in moral issues 'I just *must* do so-and-so', or (like Luther) 'I can do no other': and this sort of language expresses our subservience to psychological compulsion, not the firmness of rational decision. We are, indeed, all slaves to our own compulsions and prejudices: but we do not have to surrender to them unconditionally and *in toto*. We can at least remain intellectually clear about our situation, and fight on the right side.

Unless this point is first grasped, any other advice would be mere whistling in the dark. If we want to adopt a more rational attitude, there are all sorts of ways in which we can be helped to do so, and all sorts of temptations which we must avoid. To begin with a point which perhaps applies particularly to more sophisticated or intellectual people, we must not use ethical criteria of an academic, pseudo-philosophical kind. Since there is no question of proof or logical compulsion in the acceptance of ultimate ethical criteria, there is little value in constructing equations such as 'what is good = what makes for happiness', 'what is good = what satisfies the conscience', and so on, if such equations are intended to settle the matter once and for all. For either they become tautological, and useless as practical guides; or else they seem arbitrary: for why *must* we think that happiness is always good, or that what satisfies the conscience always right? Moreover—and this is perhaps the more important point—these quick and facile solutions to the problem are bound to fail, not simply because they are capable of logical ambiguity, but because there is no one problem and hence no one solution. For if we are right in holding that the proper acceptance of criteria depends on the proper understanding of human nature and human purposes, it is clear that our task will be largely a matter of hard work and patient discovery, not a treasure hunt with only one prize. We must look at the facts, because there is nothing else a rational person can look at. This is an obvious truth, whose simplicity is only obscured by a misunderstanding of Moralist metaphysic and Moralist purposes: a misunderstanding which I hope to have cleared up in the last chapter. Since there is no quick way to decide which ethical criteria can properly be accepted, a rational person can only consider the facts and choose without prejudice: indeed, the notion of rationality is partly defined by the willingness to do this. Hence to ask for an ultimate reason for a moral choice is, in effect, to ask whether a rational person in full possession of the facts would regard such a course as satisfactory.

Unfortunately we are by no means free from the sort of logical cheating which modern philosophers have castigated in the works of their predecessors. There is always the temptation for thinkers to thrust their moral values on the public by unfair means: usually either by trying to make them appear logically inevitable, or by giving them a false backing of expert authority. It is doubly unfortunate that this unfairness is today chiefly found in the writings of psychologists, who should be busy discovering facts for other people to look at rather than telling them how they ought to live. The logical sleight-of-hand consists of taking a phrase which carries a strong implication of value, such as 'mental health' or 'sanity', and then trying to cash it in terms of phrases in which there is still some element of value, but in which the descriptive element is far stronger, such as 'maturity', 'adjustment', or 'responsible behaviour'. It is then very easy for the reader to cash these last phrases in purely descriptive terms: we all know what a 'mature' or 'adjusted' person is like—someone who is contented in his job, who is a good mixer, who remains faithful to his wife, who accepts the limitations of his life without fretting too much, and so on. We are thus led to make the transfer from 'mental health' (which we all want) to being good mixers, being faithful to our wives, etc. (which perhaps we did not all want to do before reading the argument): and the transfer is the more plausible, since the psychologist-author is presumed to be an expert on 'mental health'.

This is a very old trick, but still a very common one: the modern psychologists have taken it over from the ancient moral philosophers. Instead of Plato leading us gently from 'justice' to 'each man doing his proper job', and thence to the caste-system of the Republic, we now have psychologists leading us from 'mental health', via 'adjustment', to the acceptance of those moral standards and behaviour-patterns which our present society professes— and which may be just as undesirable as we think Plato's caste-system to be. There are hundreds of words whose descriptive and evaluative elements can be stressed as and when it suits the authorities to do so—'patient', 'deviate', 'abnormal', 'adult', 'neurotic', and so forth. All these are commonly used—and not only by psychologists—to browbeat the public into accepting a scheme of values which it is not given a fair chance to assess. There are no doubt many reasons for this: first, a universal desire to make others believe what you believe; second, the general pressure towards conformity which is common at this period of history, and is perhaps our age's version of Moralism; third, there are the psychological discoveries

which are sufficient to make the words used seem plausible
—for doubtless there are plenty of cases where words like
'immature' or 'maladjusted' are justifiable, both as
descriptive terms and as pejorative ones, just as phrases
like 'malignant tumour' or 'malformation of the spine'
are justifiable in the vocabulary of physical medicine. But
the temptation to abuse these terms must be strenuously
resisted: the more so since psychology is our chief tool for
the discovery of facts about human beings. Psychologists,
social workers, marriage guidance counsellors and all
others in this field would do well to limit their ambitions.
There are, after all, plenty of jobs they can still do.[1]

But it is not only high-level, large-scale criteria which
are doctrinaire. A rational approach to morality involves
accepting that *all* criteria not derived solely from the
facts are doctrinaire. The most widely held doctrinaire
criteria are Moralist in nature: a great many people hold
firmly and uncritically to values supposed absolute and
a priori, such as the value of justice, equality, keeping
promises, not taking human life, and so forth. The authority
of such principles and rules is generally unchallenged,
and so far as most people are concerned this authority is
not based on a study of the facts. The intervention of
such Moralist principles forms the chief distraction from
any rational approach. But we may also be misled by
criteria, which may originally have been Factualist
criteria, but which can now be seen not to fit all the facts.
Thus it is a gross over-simplification, from the viewpoint of
depth psychology, to say that all men primarily seek
pleasure or happiness: and if we set these up as our criteria we
shall find them equally doctrinaire and equally misleading.

[1] The point made here is very well documented in Lady Wootton's book,
Social Science and Social Pathology (Allen and Unwin, 1959).

Further, by refusing to tie ourselves down to doctrinaire criteria, we find our attention drawn away from the acceptance of any supposedly objective or absolute values, and directed towards the process and conditions of moral choice itself. It is *our own choosing* which is important rather than any external 'values'. Thus it is plain that the most important facts we have to learn are facts about ourselves, for without these we cannot choose rationally. It is often supposed that we can extricate ourselves from all our moral difficulties by taking two consecutive steps: first, by identifying 'the good', or finding out what is really right and wrong; and second, by tapping some source of power that will enable us to live up to the ideals that we have discovered—by cultivating a sense of duty, for instance, or seeking the help of God. This whole process is fundamentally misconceived. Unless we are clear about ourselves and our own motives, the moral criteria we accept are likely to be largely our own inventions, in the sense that they are more likely to fit features of our own minds about which we are ignorant than to fit the facts of the real world. In these circumstances it is no wonder that we find it difficult to live up to our ideals, since the ideals are likely to conflict both with the external world and with other parts of our own nature which we have failed to take into account.

The cases mentioned earlier, where our willpower fails, or we become distracted from the facts, or lack the emotional maturity to adopt a neutral agnosticism, are all cases of a failure of self-knowledge. It is important to realise that self-knowledge is not merely something which is desirable in general (as everyone would admit), but a necessary methodological feature for anyone who wants rational certainty in morals. It is not just a useful tool for a fuller and happier life: it is an integral part of any moral philosophy which is supposed to be at once rational and at the same time not too remote from ordinary living. By describing the sort of language-situation in which we *ought* to find ourselves when facing moral problems—a situation in which we consider the facts, avoid doctrinaire principles, eschew Moralism, and so on—we thereby place ourselves, as rational beings, under the necessity of making ourselves *able* to meet this situation. To describe the situation clearly and to distinguish it from other situations is of considerable help: but it is insufficient, if only because different people find different obstacles standing in the way of their capacity to adopt a rational approach. The only general directive that can be given in this context is the directive to acquire self-knowledge. Like the general methodological criterion of 'what fits the facts', this directive is not as vacuous as it may sound. It stands in contrast to other directives which might be given, such as 'search your conscience' or 'try harder'. These directives do fit the context of certain Moralist language-situations; but in the context of considering moral problems rationally it is self-awareness which is important.

It is also possible to describe a rational approach in sociological terms. Briefly, a methodology based on looking at the facts means that we must face moral issues not as judges or policemen, but rather as educationalists or psychologists. The situation calls for a clinical approach, not a Moralist one. A good educationalist should display all the features of a rational approach which we have mentioned, and others as well. He will not be doctrinaire, but will consider each case on its own merits, looking at the facts (rather than at any moral principles) in an endeavour to do the best he can for each particular person with whom he has to deal. He will be well aware that he has to watch himself most carefully, to avoid any kind of prejudice or partisanship which might detract from the wisdom of his decisions about other people. Such principles as he has will be evolved in the course of long experience, not held *a priori*: and they will be extremely flexible. He will not allow his thinking to be dominated by Moralist language, but will nearly always content himself with considering the facts, and posing the very general question 'What is the best thing to do in this particular case?' He may find certain generalisations to have wide application: for instance, he may find himself often considering how to preserve individual freedom, or the integration of the community, or the appearance of justice, or confidence in his own administration. But these principles will not be absolute, and will always be subordinated to his treatment of each case on its merits. They will be regarded as important factors in the situation, but not as dominating it.

It is in the highest degree unfortunate that for so many people the notions of a 'rational morality' and of 'looking at the facts' suggest a dry, unfeeling approach to life. For this philosophers are partly to blame: they have not generally succeeded in showing clearly how such an approach can, in fact, lead to a far more sympathetic and a far fuller moral life than the life most of us are accustomed to lead at present. For to learn about something is also to learn to love it. The desire to look at the facts engenders understanding and interest, which in turn engender sympathy and love—the desire to do what is best for a person, rather than merely to treat him according to doctrinaire principles not based on understanding. Many of our attitudes towards our fellows masquerade as altruistic: but

171

if they are not based on understanding they are likely to do more harm than good. There is no tyrant so dangerous as the tyrant who thinks he is a benevolent despot.

The chief skill required in trying to adopt the role of an understanding helper and friend is the ability to communicate with our fellows. There are two reasons for this, both of vital importance. First, since no psychological text-book can tell us all the facts we need to know about every particular case, it is essential to improve our own perceptivity and awareness of other people, so that we may know their needs. This cannot be done in isolation, but only in the context of close communication, freed as far as possible from any kind of conceptual confusion or psychological disturbance. Second, we need the communication and understanding of our fellow men, in order that we ourselves may be helped to be rational. Here too isolation is fatal: we need the constant intercourse of thought and feeling to keep us aware of ourselves and our difficulties. Progress is not made in ivory towers, but by the cut-and-thrust of debate, the mutual assistance of collaborators, and the support and sympathy of friends.

This process calls for the practice of certain virtues, which are not in every case those normally associated with morality. They are, indeed, more usually considered the virtues of the successful scientist. It is not primarily the qualities of integrity, willpower, or intellectual brilliance which are in demand here: emphasis should rather be placed on patience, honesty with ourselves, humility, and calmly serious approach—almost a professional approach—to moral problems. Intellectual pyrotechnics are not called for, and intellectual brilliance is of no value without close contact with other people, so that it is at once of use to them, and at the same time less likely to run wild through the lack of the natural checks and balances of intercommunication. Our willpower and determination must be largely transferred from their present purposes and put to work in the service of adopting a rational approach. We now try too hard to live up to moral principles of whose validity we have no secure knowledge, and not hard enough to approach morality in the right way. The possibility of progress in rational morality, with all the practical consequences in political and other fields for which we hope so ardently, depends to a very large extent on making this transference.

Such an approach to morality would, indeed, mean the end of morality as we know it. Our society, like all others, has delimited morality in certain ways: for one reason or another, some issues are moral issues with us and other issues are not. But this delimitation has not been arrived at by a study of the facts, and hence carries no special authority. The study of human nature and human purposes would give us the chance to make a genuinely objective assessment of those features which are of outstanding importance: so that if we wish to take some issues more seriously than others, we shall have good grounds for choosing which issues they are to be. Since morality will be concerned with human nature as a whole, we should presumably choose those features of human nature and experience which are of outstanding causative importance. Thus, if it turns out to be true that the way in which parents punish their children has an immense effect on the children's lives, this would be regarded as immensely important—though in many societies the question is left to the discretion of the parents, and not regarded in a very serious light. Conversely, if it turns out to be true that the sexual expression of each individual is not a matter of outstanding importance to him or to society, this would be regarded as largely a matter of taste or personal discretion—though in nearly all societies it is now regarded as a very serious moral issue. We cannot tell what the facts will show. At present we are merely stumbling in the dark, vastly ignorant both of ourselves and our fellow men. To recognise this in ethics, as we have recognised it in science, is the first step to be taken.

3. EPILOGUE

This is perhaps more like sociology than philosophy, and may seem merely a dim modern reflection of the nineteenth-century utilitarian dream, wherein philosophy drops out of the race, and the social sciences take over. But we should now be able to see clearly that this sort of departmentalisation will not do. When the philosopher studies language, his enquiry is necessarily a sociological one—even though he may not choose to take it very far. Unfortunately philosophy is still largely content to live upon the considerable capital amassed by Wittgenstein and others. The tendency has been to imply, or tacitly assume, that morality-games and other games are self-contained and self-guaranteeing; that all the philosopher can do is to publish the games, as it were: to separate them carefully, put the whole compendium in a box, and write formal instructions on the lid about the rules relating to each. But there are other instructions you can write on the lid besides formal ones: instructions like 'A good family game for young and old', or 'This game sharpens the wits and requires considerable concentration'.

After having described in a general, non-formal way the manner in which facts and the acceptance of criteria interlock in real life, we can now see in what ways a purely formal study of moral language may mislead. The classical philosophers, insufficiently conscious of the necessity for such study, tended to assimilate value to fact, and value-words to empirical language. 'Good' means 'giving pleasure': 'justice' means 'everyone doing his proper job'; or if they do not exactly mean these things, they ought to mean them; or anyway, we can take it that it is so. Or perhaps an identification is made: goodness *is* the quality of giving pleasure: justice *is* everyone doing his proper job. However we interpret this sort of programme, our objection is that it forces the issue too much: that it does not leave it open to us to change our criteria, to guide ourselves towards satisfaction in other ways than those the philosopher recommends. We don't like Plato's state: and Plato has added insult to injury by employing the word 'justice', so that it takes a lot of work to lift it out of the monopoly he has made, and use it for our own purposes. A philosopher's objection would be differently phrased: he would say that 'justice' does not in normal usage mean what Plato makes it mean, that evaluative language is of a different kind from descriptive language, that you cannot derive an 'ought' from an 'is', and so forth. But the sociological point is perhaps the more significant. We don't want the issue forced in this way. We want to keep our evaluative language evaluative, free from attempts to tie it down to empirical facts. This is because we are not satisfied that we have got all the facts we need: even if we agree, we should not feel happy about agreeing. Nevertheless we want to agree: only we want to agree freely, not to have other people's values shoved down our throats. By contrast, some modern philosophers tend to regard evaluative language purely as fulfilling formal functions in a game. This must be so, they think, because how can there be normative language without a norm? 'Good' operates 'like an imperative', 'like a decision', 'like any grading work'. 'Right' must always refer to criteria of rightness. But this is also a mistake. There must be words which refer to the body of rules as a whole, rather than to the operations we perform within a framework of rules; and we should naturally expect 'good' and 'right' to have uses of this kind. It must be possible to say 'This is a good game' as well as 'This is a good card to play in the game'.

Once we drop the game metaphor, or at least add to it, we can see how this must obviously be true. Awareness that language is related to social factors suggests that, unlike a game, it is not wholly reducible to cut-and-dried, self-contained systems. It is like an institution rather than a machine: it can grow or change, has certain ends dimly or half-consciously in view, looks for new criteria and new rules rather than simply obeying existing ones. Questions like 'Is this *really* good?' or 'Is that *really* right?' ask for sociological as well as logical guidance: they are not to be stifled by repeatedly pointing out the existing criteria. They are much more like the demands: 'Is this really what I want?', 'Will this really bring satisfaction?' So too with the question 'Is it really true?', which may not be satisfied by a prolonged and careful demonstration of empirical facts coupled with an examination of the appropriate criteria. Certainly, some things must be true—in some languages. But the demand is really 'What happens if I use this language?' or 'Is this whole game worth playing?' Words like 'good' are used in statements to endorse not only particular events or propositions, but also whole institutions and other forms of life in which events or propositions occur: just as we can endorse, disclaim or hesitate about cheques made out not only to individuals but to groups of individuals.

The behaviour of language is formally like a game: but in other respects it is far more like a slice of real life. There are times in life when we abide by the rules, so to speak: when we act sensibly and purposively, using those means and instruments which we possess to fulfil our ends: when we act by agreed criteria, and are not worried. But there are also times when we sit and sulk, or are depressed, or lose our tempers, or wonder what to do. We have doubts: some of these may be straightforward doubts about the facts; but others—and there will be a great many others— are neurotic doubts, cases where our general method of living is somehow unsatisfactory, where accepted criteria break down and we seek new ones in a vague, semi-conscious haze of dissatisfaction. It is here that we need analysis and clarification: that is, we need a clear demonstration and understanding of our own purposes. The philosopher tackles our linguistic behaviour much as a kind friend (or, if we can afford one, a kind psychoanalyst) might tackle our behaviour. He talks round the centre of the trouble, brings up the same points again and again, clarifies, elucidates and gives us *consciousness* of what we are doing, together with an understanding and a sense of proportion about the situation we are actually in. After much talk, if it is successful, the patient is really content. He has not been bullied into anything, but he has a feeling of having 'worked through' all the points, so that he can now feel free to do what he wants.

We must thus equally avoid the mistakes of somehow forcing the individual to accept criteria he really does not want to accept, as the classical philosophers tried to do, and of assuming that the criteria which he professes are actually satisfactory for him. There is an illuminating parallel here in political theory. One mistake in politics is to force the issue too much for a government—to present it with a highly detailed blue-print or a complicated written constitution, and insist that the government follows it in every respect. But it is equally a mistake to assume that any game which a government plays is satisfactory—even granted that it is composed of altruistic, sensible individuals whose one object is to give public service. There are times when we are prepared to play by the standard rules, particularly if we wish to preserve continuity of administration: but there are also times when we want to challenge the rules. Accepted language-patterns, like accepted moral concepts in Moralism, act primarily as conservative forces both in the individual and in society: and a challenge to the accepted patterns is a challenge to individual and social life.

The existence of the parallel with governmental administration is not a pure coincidence. We might say that the administration is the super-ego of the community. One of its main desires is to preserve order, just as the main function of the super-ego in the individual is to preserve order, and to prevent him from dislocation or fragmentation. The administration to some extent represses, and to some extent yields, when faced with the wills of various individuals or groups within the state: it tries to preserve a balance, to avoid trouble, and to secure cohesion. The super-ego, and the Moralist concepts and language-games which stem from it, have the same function, which is to allow the expression of id-desires and id-energy only so far as is compatible with the integration of the whole personality. The clarification of language by the philosopher is parallel to the freedom of the press—to the general procedure of making public what sort of game the government is playing at any time—which acts as a kind of psychoanalysis of the state. The object in each case, again like the object of psychoanalysis, is to promote the maximum of consciousness—even, in a sense, of conflict— consistent with integration.

This parallel should show us that there is an important sense in which philosophy is not neutral as regards practical behaviour. It is certainly neutral in the sense that it does not attempt to use any kind of force or bullying for or against one side or the other: it simply clarifies. But the word 'simply' is misleading. To clarify, to make unconscious behaviour of any kind conscious, to make people think, is essentially to side with the forces of change and to threaten, however indirectly or unwillingly, the forces of conservatism. Proper philosophy, like proper psychoanalysis, is *disturbing*. It is disturbing in exactly the way it might disturb the government of a country if all its administrative and foreign policies were really exposed to public view. For instance, there is no doubt that there are many administrative contexts in which the administrators are employed in blocking, braking or positively stifling the popular will. If they stated that they were playing this game every time they played it, or even if it were widely known that the game was played at all, it could hardly be played so successfully: and it is arguable that the continuity and stability of the administration might suffer in consequence. In the same way, it is much more difficult for men to moralise if they know that they are playing some of the Moralist games to which we referred—the game of reinforcing moral concepts, making certain people feel disloyal, and so forth. This increased awareness forces upon them the necessity of *acting*, if they are going to play the game at all. They have to pretend; and then it is not quite the game that it once was.

It seems, then, either disingenuous or stupid for philosophers to protest that they are in every sense neutral. As conservatives always say, they do not 'leave well alone'. They upset people in exact proportion to their effectiveness. One might even say, with an air of paradox, that they upset people in exact proportion to their reasonableness: for the picture of reason or clarity as a wholly conservative, peace-engendering force is mythical. Reason is a revolutionary force, and 'human kind cannot bear very much reality'. It is too easy to paint a picture of idealists like Socrates, fighting for freedom and always wickedly repressed by the forces of prejudice and convention: as if such people wished only to be left alone, only to think and talk freely, and not to take part in any kind of struggle other than at an academic level. Such may be their intentions: but such is not the effect of what they do. A question has the sociological force of an attack.

Philosophers, then, are engaged in a sociological war whether they like it or not; and it is incumbent on them to realise this, and to guide their actions accordingly. Since this is inevitable, since total quietism is out of the question, it can hardly be regarded as unfortunate. It has simply got to be faced: just as a schoolmaster, for instance, has to face the question of whether he should encourage, allow, or directly prevent his boys from reading critical works on sex, psychology, class conflict, Communism, and so forth. Any schoolmaster knows that this is a real problem; by encouraging questions and criticism he is taking risks with the integration of the community which he governs, and by quietly discouraging it, so far as possible, he *ipso facto* helps to preserve the values and continuity of his administration. Naturally, if he is at all interested in promoting awareness and clarity, he will be prepared to compromise the integration of the community to some extent. He may find that much of the fear of questioning and clarification is neurotic: that it is in fact quite possible to preserve integration without a façade of deliberately unquestioned values and morality-games. He may also find that those boys whose loyalty might, indeed, be too much affected by clarification are also those who are incapable of it. These two saving clauses, which operate in other communities besides schools, may perhaps be thought to save the philosopher and other reasoners from overmuch anxiety about the effects of their actions.

There are plenty of other reasons why philosophers should not worry too much about this situation. First, the uncritical and unaware may well suffer from disturbances of their own which clarification might cure: just as an excessively strong or misdirected super-ego may produce neurotic disturbances for the psychoanalyst to cure. Secondly, we might think that the principle of freedom of thought, freedom to consider only truth and not political or psychological expediency, to be so important and so likely to perish amid the forces of unreason that we should accept almost any amount of disturbance in order to safeguard it. And lastly, of course, if philosophers cannot pursue truth without interference from their own anxiety about the effect of truth, then who can? Philosophers are not politicians: and the politicians will interfere only too soon, if they think that integration is too much threatened. Nobody *has* to buy books on philosophy, and nobody is compelled to attend university lectures and tutorials which may shatter his faith and morals (and how often does this happen, anyway?).

Reason and Morals

I myself believe that we can use very much more reason and clarification in all fields—the philosophical, psychological—without undue damage; and I have brought forward these concluding considerations chiefly in order to show how very far from the truth is the accepted picture of the modern moral philosopher as a dry, sterile neutral— as a sociological neuter, we might say. So far from having finished with the lives and behaviour of ordinary people, modern philosophy has hardly started to probe, order and transform them. The methodology outlined in this chapter, if it were indeed accepted, would certainly promote changes on a vast scale. It is not, perhaps, the philosopher's business to worry about whether changes of this sort will be sociologically beneficial; but he need not be modest about owning up to them. Better to admit, honestly, that you are on the side of revolution than to profess, dishonestly, that you are not even trying to cut any ice at all.

The ordinary man has not yet had what he is entitled to expect from philosophers. To outline a methodology, as I have tried to do in this book, is only to have indicated a general direction, not to have given an exact compass-bearing, much less to have made a precise route-map: yet he cannot expect more exactitude from us. But if the general direction is right, he is entitled to ask how he may follow it. One might say: 'Well, just *go*.' But somehow this seems rather abrupt, and conveys the impression, which I complained of earlier, that the philosopher has finished with him. And this is a false picture: knowing how to do ethics properly is not like knowing which way to go. Being able to think clearly is a gradually acquired skill. The plain man may ask how he is to acquire more of it. Again we can give an abrupt answer: 'Practice.' But what sort of practice is best, how can he get the practice?

This isn't a silly question, and it isn't one the philosopher can just shrug off. Remarks that philosophers are fond of making, like 'This is a question for educationalists'; or 'This is a question of psychology', are just a little too slick. They form part of a language-game whose purposes must not be taken at their face value. Apparently the purpose of the game is a methodological one: the assertions point us towards the department of knowledge that ought to be able to answer our question. But, in view of the fact that educationalists and psychologists may not attempt to answer questions of which philosophers say 'This is a question for educationalists or psychologists', the game seems to have another purpose—to shrug off the questions, so that philosophers need not commit themselves in any way by answering them. It may also serve the purpose of stimulating educationalists and psychologists to answer them; and of course this is highly desirable. But in fact they still fail to do so. It does not seem unreasonable, therefore, to suggest that philosophers might take up the work: rather, perhaps, as a parish priest in the past might have done jobs of which he could have said 'There really ought to be doctors to do this', or 'This needs a trained teacher'.

Moreover, it is doubtful whether the frontiers of the different disciplines are really so clear-cut. The ordinary man on the road to philosophy may find himself in a sort of no-man's land, where he is continually thrust back by jealous frontier guards on both sides. For after all, what do we really expect psychologists to *do* about it? Certainly, they may be able to heal us so that we have the urge and the energy to think straight, to remove our anxieties and compulsions so that we are able to practise. But the practising has still to be done. One can be quite sane, and still be no good at philosophy (and vice versa). We can turn to the educationalists (*are* there such people, really?) and the teachers should be able to help us. But this is to be bewitched by the word 'teach': not all teachers can teach people how to do all subjects. The teachers of philosophy, then? Yes; but aren't these the philosophers?

If philosophers were to admit their sociological function, they might become less unpopular: or at least, unpopular in a different way. For it is the general tone of modern philosophy, rather than its particular precepts, which bores or infuriates the ordinary man. Philosophers fail to realise that there are quite a lot of people who are against reason, at least in the sense that philosophers are for it. The ordinary man does not admire neutrality and objectivity: he wants to be asked to join a party or believe in a creed, even if he does not choose to accept the invitation. He gets angry if there is no party and no creed, in the way that a neurotic gets angry when you tell him to make up his own mind, instead of telling him what to do. If philosophy is therapeutic or educational, then philosophers must stand out clearly as therapists or teachers: otherwise there is an important sense in which they would not be taking their job seriously. People might then be slightly more annoyed by their apparent presumption, but they would certainly be less annoyed by their remoteness. There are few things more irritating than being patronised.

A full realisation of their role as teachers would, I believe, cause philosophers to make some important changes in their methods and their programme. For the person being taught must be taken seriously, as well as the process of teaching: just as in psychoanalysis it is the patient that counts as well as the psychological theory. At present philosophers tend to presuppose a norm of rationality and models of rational method which do not fit the ordinary man—and it is still unclear whether and in what sense they ought to fit him. But plainly this must not be the only approach for a subject which is really a kind of conceptual psychoanalysis, and not a fact-gathering subject. Clarification is not an abstract activity, but an educational one which involves a relationship between people: and what clarifies for one man obscures for another. For these reasons it is plainly important that philosophers should familiarise themselves with the speech and life of ordinary people, with their linguistic rituals and their social activities, with their prejudices and their passions. How ordinary people actually argue, how we can help them to think, how far their beliefs can be usefully described in logical terms and how far in psychological terms—these are some of the questions which must be asked if the revolution in philosophy is ever to have more than academic importance.

BIBLIOGRAPHY

The following is a brief list of works which the reader might find useful in connection with the present book:

J. C. Flugel, *Man, Morals and Society* (Pelican Books).

H. and H. A. Frankfort, *Before Philosophy* (Pelican Books).

Stuart Hampshire, *Thought and Action* (Chatto and Windus).

R. M. Hare, *The Language of Morals* (O.U.P.).

D. M. Mackinnon, *A Study of Ethical Theory* (A. and C. Black).

P. H. Nowell-Smith, *Ethics* (Pelican Books).

Stephen Toulmin, *The Place of Reason in Ethics* (C.U.P.).

John Wilson, *Language and the Pursuit of Truth* (C.U.P.).

John Wisdom, *Philosophy and Psychoanalysis* (Blackwell).

L. Wittgenstein, *Philosophical Investigations* (Blackwell).

INDEX

Aristotle, 60, 71, 96, 97
Ayer, A. J., 24

Britton, Karl, 136

cause and effect in human behaviour, 46–56
certainty, demand for in ethics, 19–31
criteria
  in empirical knowledge, 139–46
  purposes lying behind the adoption of criteria, 146–8
  agreement about ethical criteria, 149–55
  dangers of ultimate ethical criteria, 165

equality, 98–9

Factualism, the Factualist approach to morals, 38 f.
freedom
  logical analysis of, 57 f.
  social value of, 123–9
Flugel, J. C., 100
Freud, S., 15, 48
Frankfort, H., 48

Gellner, Ernest, 1

Hampshire, Stuart, 55, 59
Huxley, Aldous, 104, 127

Kant, E., 131, 161

language-games, 106, 119–20, 174–7
Lawrence, D. H., 15, 34–5
Lucas, J. R., 120

merit and desert, 93 f.
miracles, 52–3

morality
  delimitation of the area of morality, 80–2, 173–4
  conflicts between groups or individuals, 156–9
  Moralism as an approach to morals, 38 f.
  moral principles (loyalty, honesty, etc.), 83 f.
  authority in moral thinking, 40–2
  sexual morality, 39, 81, 161, 173–4
moral philosophy, modern
  dullness of, 1–2, 18, 34–5
  points established by, 19–24
  comparison with psychoanalysis, 15–18, 177–9
  social function of, 177–85

Nowell-Smith, P. H., 2, 3, 24, 26, 70, 76

pacifism, 112
Plato, 8, 64, 86, 151, 159, 167, 175
praise and blame, 71 f.
predictability, 46–56, 58
psychologists, unfair persuasion by, 166–8

'reasonable' as a concept in morality, 31–5
religion in connection with Moralism, 112, 117, 120–1
retribution, 96 f.

self, the, 64–70, 80–1
self-awareness, importance of to morality, 169–70
Socrates, 180

'trying' as a concept in morality, 55

Wittgenstein, L., 9, 48, 106
Wootton, Barbara, 168

187